IDENTIFYING GIFTED STUDENTS

a practical guide

IDENTIFYING GIFTED STUDENTS

a practical guide

edited by
SUSAN K. JOHNSEN

a joint publication with the
TEXAS ASSOCIATION FOR THE GIFTED AND TALENTED

PRUFROCK PRESS, INC.

Printed in the United States of America.

ISBN 1-59363-003-4

At the time of this book's publication, all facts and figures cited are the most current available. All telephone numbers, addresses, and Web site URLs are accurate and active. All publications, organizations, Web sites, and other resources exist as described in the book, and all have been verified. The authors and Prufrock Press, Inc., make no warranty or guarantee concerning the information and materials given out by organizations or content found at Web sites, and we are not responsible for any changes that occur after this book's publication. If you find an error, please contact Prufrock Press, Inc. We strongly recommend to parents, teachers, and other adults that you monitor children's use of the Internet.

Prufrock Press, Inc.
P.O. Box 8813
Waco, Texas 76714-8813
(800) 998-2208
Fax (800) 240-0333
http://www.prufrock.com

TABLE OF CONTENTS

LIST OF TABLES & FIGURES

Overview of Assessment

by Susan K. Johnsen

Assessment is the process of gathering information using appropriate tests, instruments, and techniques. The information is gathered for a specific purpose such as screening, classification or selection, curriculum planning or diagnosis, program planning, and progress evaluation.

This book, *Identifying Gifted Students: A Practical Guide*, focuses on screening and selecting gifted and talented students. It is designed for practicing professionals—teachers, counselors, psychologists, and administrators—who must make decisions daily about identifying and serving gifted and talented students.

The book is intended to be relevant in any state or setting that uses multiple assessments to identify gifted students within an increasingly diverse population. Because the book is a joint publication with the Texas Association for the Gifted and Talented, many of the examples illustrate issues faced by Texas K-12 programs as they implement compliance standards in the State of Texas

In organizing the book, the following sequential set of steps in the identification process was considered:

Step 1. Identify the characteristics of gifted and talented students and program options.

Step 2. Select multiple assessments that match these characteristics and programs.

Step 3. Develop an identification procedure—nomination, screening, and selection—that ensures equal access for all populations.

Step 4. Provide professional development for administrators and teachers.

Step 5. Provide an orientation for parents and interested community members.

Step 6. Administer assessments.

Step 7. Interpret results and place gifted and talented students in best program options.

Step 8. Evaluate and revise assessment procedures.

Chapter One reviews the definitions, models, and characteristics of gifted and talented students (i.e., Step 1 in the identification process). Definitions include the 1993 federal definition from the U.S. Department of Education and the closely aligned Texas definition. Given the focus on "capability" or "potential," two developmental models were chosen, one by Françoys Gagné and one by Abraham Tannenbaum, both of which emphasize the importance of other factors that contribute to the development of "gifts" into "talents." Given these models, identification becomes even more important in ensuring that each student is impacted by positive environmental and intrapersonal catalysts and learns how to become aware of and use "chance" factors as they appear throughout his or her life. These models are followed by lists of characteristics for each defined area that have been gleaned from assessment instruments, introductory texts, and research. The chapter concludes by focusing on characteristics of hard-to-find gifted and talented students, which should encourage practitioners to cast a wide net in the identification process.

In Chapter Two, Gail Ryser explains approaches to qualitative and quantitative assessments, defining differences and providing types. Three of the most widely used qualitative assessments—portfolios, interviews, and observations—are discussed in greater depth with specific examples. With quantitative assessments, she defines norm- and criterion-referenced measures along with achievement, aptitude, and intelligence tests. She then reviews reliability and validity issues and emphasizes that technical qualities must be addressed when using either qualitative or quantitative assessments.

In Chapter Three, the discussion of important characteristics of selecting instruments is continued with the examination of culture-fair and nonbiased assessment. Ryser initially examines barriers that tend to exclude students from programs for gifted students, including negative attitudes toward minority students, exclusive definitions, and tests that are not fair to diverse gifted students. The chapter then presents strategies that can be used to overcome these barriers.

In Chapter Four, Jennifer Jolly and Jennifer Robins Hall supply the technical information for more than 40 assessments that are frequently used in gifted education. Using either the technical manual or other reviews, they examine the purpose of the test, validity, reliability, age of the instrument, the norming sample, types of scores, administration format, and qualifications of testing personnel. Given the importance of up-to-date norms due to changing demographics, they excluded any assessments whose norms were older than 10 years. They also have provided handy information for practitioners, including publisher addresses, an alphabetic listing and summary table of all reviewed tests, and a separate review for each test. Chapters Two, Three, and Four should provide practitioners with the necessary data for selecting multiple assessments that match gifted and talented student characteristics and programs (Step 2) and provide important information for the development of professionals who will be involved in the identification process.

Chapter Five will be particularly helpful for districts that have tentatively selected a set of assessments and are in the process of developing an identification procedure. The chapter begins with a review of the importance of using multiple criteria. Besides legal and compliance issues, multiple assessments provide excellent opportunities for students to demonstrate outstanding performance in a variety of settings to a variety of important others such as friends, teachers, and parents. Each phase of the identification process—nomination, screening, and selection—is then described, with additional attention paid to the appeals and due process procedures. The remainder of the chapter focuses on organizing data for decision making and interpreting the results. Five guidelines provide criteria for evaluating forms that might be used in summarizing data: weighting of assessments, comparable scores, error in measures, best performance, and descriptions of the student. Following the discussion of each of these guidelines, the chapter supplies three sample forms for organizing data: case study, profile, and minimum scores.

The final chapter helps school districts understand the process of evaluation. It discusses six components: key features, data sources and instrument review, methods and measurement options, data interpretation, the report, and recommendations. While emphasis is placed on the evaluation of identification procedures, this chapter provides a framework for evaluating other features of the gifted and talented program.

We would like to thank the Texas Association for the Gifted and Talented for giving us this opportunity to revise the previous TAGT monograph on identification and all of the editorial assistance from Prufrock Press, particularly Jim Kendrick. We hope that you find this book helpful in establishing procedures that are effective in identifying gifted and talented students.

CHAPTER ONE

Definitions, Models, and Characteristics of Gifted Students

by Susan K. Johnsen

A ndrea is a kindergarten child, full of energy and excitement like most children her age except that she is already reading at a fourth-grade level and understands mathematics concepts at a fifth-grade level. She likes to play games with the other children in her classroom, but she is interested in black holes, a topic most children her age don't understand. Since she is social, she has established a learning center about black holes for other children in her kindergarten classroom and has become the editor of a schoolwide newsletter. While very accomplished for a 6-year-old child, Andrea is quite humble about her prodigious abilities and appears to enjoy each day with her classmates.

* * *

After failing two grades in his elementary school, Burton is 13 and has finally made it to the sixth grade. While Burton doesn't turn in much work, his sixth-grade teacher has noticed that he seems to have a mathematical mind and catches on to new concepts easily. In fact, he aced a nationally normed analogies test and enjoyed talking about how each of the items was designed. His friends know that he has built a working roller coaster in his back yard out of scrap lumber and electronic equipment. However, because of his lack of interest in grades and schoolwork, the teacher did not refer Burton to the gifted and talented program because he doesn't do the work that will prepare him for the mandated state test.

* * *

Ryan, a high school student, is a challenge for his parents and teachers alike. It's not unusual for him to wear Christmas lights to school to attract attention from his favorite girlfriend, to dye his hair several colors, or to wear red gloves to a band concert. Although he scores well on national tests, recently making a 1350 on his SAT, he performs at a minimal level in his classes and is not even in the top 10%. He loves music, playing three different instruments proficiently: the tuba, the cello, and the bass guitar. Outside of school, he has organized and leads two jazz bands, recently cutting his first CD. The summer following his senior year, he has been accepted to the Drum Corps International before beginning college.

Definitions

These three vignettes based on true stories describe children who are gifted and talented. While not always in school, each one has particular abilities that are manifested in a variety of ways—one through his music and leadership, another through his reasoning and constructions, and the third through academic performance. Andrea's teachers would clearly identify her as gifted and talented, but Burton and Ryan might not be selected because of their lack of interest in school. They are indeed different from one another, yet they all show high performance in the areas included in the United States federal definition of gifted and talented students:

The term "gifted and talented" when used in respect to students, children, or youth means students, children, or youth who give evidence of high performance capability in areas such as intellectual, creative, artistic, or leadership capacity, or in specific academic fields, and who require services or activities not ordinarily provided by the school in order to fully develop such capabilities. (P.L. 103-382, Title XIV, p. 388)

This definition has been adopted in part or completely by the majority of the states, including Texas, whose definition states:

> In this subchapter, "gifted and talented students" means a child or youth who performs at or shows the potential for performing at a remarkably high level of accomplishment when compared to others of the same age, experience, or environment, and who:
> 1. exhibits high performance capability in an intellectual, creative, or artistic area;
> 2. possesses an unusual capacity for leadership; or
> 3. excels in a specific academic field. (74th legislature of the State of Texas, Chapter 29, Subchapter D, Section 29.121)

The major characteristics of these definitions are a) the diversity of areas in which performance may be exhibited (e.g., intellectual, creative, artistic, leadership, academic), b) the comparison with other groups (e.g., those in general education classrooms or of the same age, experience, or environment), and c) the use of terms that imply a need for development of the gift (e.g., *capability* and *potential*).

Models

This concept of "capability" or "potential" is addressed in Gagné's (1995, 1999) Differentiated Model of Giftedness and Talent (see Figure 1.1). Gagné has proposed that "gifts," which are natural abilities, must be developed to become "talents," which emerge through the systematic learning, training, and practicing "of skills characteristic of a particular field of human activity or performance" (p. 230). The development of gifts into talents may be facilitated or hindered by two types of catalysts: intrapersonal and environmental. Intrapersonal catalysts are physical (e.g., health, physical appearance) and psychological (e.g., motivation, personality, and volition), all of which are influenced by genetic background. Environmental catalysts are surroundings (e.g., geographic, demographic, sociological), people (e.g., parents, teach-

3

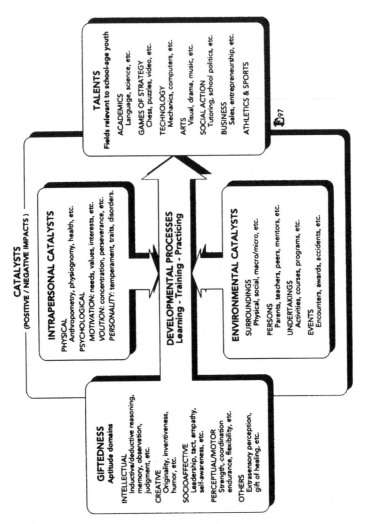

Figure 1.1. Gagné's Differentiated Model of Giftedness and Talent (DMGT)

Note. From "Is There Light at the End of the Tunnel?," by F. Gagné, 1999, *Journal for the Education of the Gifted, 22*, p. 231. Copyright ©1999 by The Association for the Gifted. Reprinted with permission.

4

ers, siblings, peers), undertakings (e.g., programs for gifted and talented students), and events (e.g., death of a parent, major illness, winning a prize). Gagné has recognized that any program that a school develops for gifted and talented students should recognize the domain or field in which it is exhibited and the level

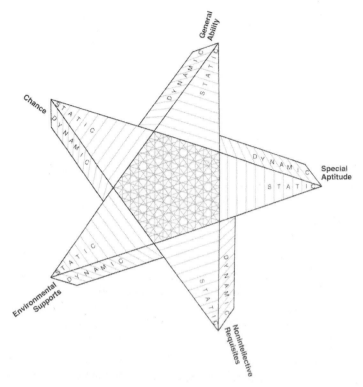

Figure 1.2. The Five Factors That "Mesh" Into Excellence

Note. From "Nature and Nuture of Giftedness" (p. 47), by A. Tannenbaum, in *Handbook of Gifted Education* (3rd ed.), N. Colangelo & G. A. Davis (Eds.), 2003, Boston: Pearson Education. Copyright ©2003 by Pearson Education. Reprinted with permission.

of the student's giftedness or talent (e.g., performing in the top 10%, 5%, 2%, 1%, or less than 1%).

Similarly, Tannenbaum (1983) viewed giftedness as an interaction of five different factors (see Figure 1.2): general ability (e.g., "g" or general intelligence), special ability (e.g., aptitude in a specific area), nonintellective facilitators (e.g., metalearning, dedication to a chosen field, strong self-concept, willingness to sacrifice, mental health), environmental influences (e.g., parents, classroom, peers, culture, social class), and chance (e.g., accidental, general exploratory, sagacity, and personalized action).

Given this importance of developing gifts into talents, school districts and the community should be involved in identifying students at an early age who exhibit characteristics in specific areas and plan their programs around these characteristics. Teachers, administrators, counselors, school psychologists, parents, siblings, peers, neighbors, and others who have contact with gifted children may assist in the nomination process if they are observant and learn about the variety of characteristics that may be exhibited in situations inside and outside of school. For example, professionals in the school may be unaware of Ryan's leadership in two jazz bands or Burton's operational roller coaster in his backyard. Parents, peers, and the gifted student need to advocate for services that will develop the potential that is apparent in these youths' areas of interest.

Characteristics

Many authors have described characteristics of gifted and talented students, some in general terms across several domains, while others have described them for specific areas cited in the federal and state definitions. Since most school districts identify children for programs that are related to the definition, this chapter organizes the characteristics according to these specific areas. Professionals who are primarily responsible for the identification process must remember that gifted and talented students *must have an opportunity to perform*. Students who are in classrooms where no differentiation is present are less likely to exhibit these characteristics. In addition, gifted and talented students will demonstrate many, but *not all*, of the characteristics that are listed in each area. In addition, gifted and talented students may show potential or performance in *only one* area. It is important that professionals, parents, and others involved in the identification process look for these characteristics over a period of time and in a variety of situations.

General Intellectual Ability

Those gifted and talented students with general intellectual ability tend to perform or show the potential to perform in several fields of study. Spearman (1923) defined this general ability as "g," which is common to many tasks. Cattell (1963) further divided "g" into *fluid* (inherited ability) and *crystallized* (abilities acquired through learning). Many general intelligence tests and checklists include items that assess both *fluid abilities*, such as analogies, block designs, and pattern arrangements, and *crystallized abilities*, such as mathematics problems, vocabulary, and comprehension of reading passages.

Researchers have consistently identified these characteristics as relating to this area (Clark, 1997; Colangelo & Davis, 1991; Coleman & Cross, 2001; Davis & Rimm, 1994; Gilliam, Carpenter, & Christensen, 1996; Khatena, 1992; Piirto, 1999; Renzulli, Smith, White, Callahan, Harman, & Westberg, 2002; Rogers, 2001; Sternberg & Davidson, 1986; Swassing, 1985; Tannenbaum, 1983):

(handwritten note in margin: general ability)

- Has an extensive and detailed memory, particularly in an area of interest.
- Has vocabulary advanced for age—precocious language.
- Has communication skills advanced for age and is able to express ideas and feelings.
- Asks intelligent questions.
- Is able to identify the important characteristics of new concepts, problems.
- Learns information quickly.
- Uses logic in arriving at common sense answers.
- Has a broad base of knowledge—a large quantity of information.
- Understands abstract ideas and complex concepts.
- Uses analogical thinking, problem solving, or reasoning.
- Observes relationships and sees connections.
- Finds and solves difficult and unusual problems.
- Understands principles, forms generalizations, and uses them in new situations.
- Wants to learn and is curious.
- Works conscientiously and has a high degree of concentration in areas of interest.
- Understands and uses various symbol systems.
- Is reflective about learning.

Specific Academic Field

In this area, gifted and talented students exhibit potential or demonstrated accomplishment in one specific field of study, such as language arts, mathematics, social studies, or science. Researchers have identified general and specific characteristics for these academic fields (Feldhusen, Hoover, & Sayler, 1990; Gilliam, Carpenter, & Christensen, 1996; Rogers, 2001; Piirto, 1999; Tannenbaum, 1983):

General (demonstrated within field of interest)

- Has an intense, sustained interest.
- Has hobbies/collections related to field.
- Attracted toward cognitive complexity, enjoys solving complex problems.
- Prefers classes/careers in the academic field.
- Is highly self-motivated, persistent.
- Has a broad base of knowledge.
- Reads widely in an academic field.
- Learns information quickly.
- Has an inquisitive nature, asks good questions.
- Examines and recalls details.
- Recognizes critical elements and details in learning concepts.
- Analyzes problems and considers alternatives.
- Understands abstract ideas and concepts.
- Uses vocabulary beyond grade level.
- Verbalizes complex concepts and processes.
- Visualizes images and translates into other forms—written, spoken, symbolic—music notation, numbers, letters.
- Sees connections and relationships in a field and generalizes to other situations, applications.

Math/Science

- Is interested in numerical analysis.
- Has a good memory for storing main features of problem and solutions.
- Appreciates parsimony, simplicity, or economy in solutions.
- Reasons effectively and efficiently.
- Solves problems intuitively using insight.
- Can reverse steps in the mental process.
- Organizes data and experiments to discover patterns or relationships.

- Improvises with science equipment and math methods.
- Is flexible in solving problems.

Social Studies/Language Arts

- Enjoys language/verbal communication, communication skills.
- Engages in intellectual play, enjoys puns, good sense of humor.
- Organizes ideas and sequences in preparation for speaking and writing.
- Suspends judgment, entertains alternative points of view.
- Is original and creative—has unique ideas in writing or speaking.
- Is sensitive to social, ethical, and moral issues.
- Is interested in theories of causation.
- Likes independent study and research in areas of interest.
- Uses these qualities in writing: paradox, parallel structure, rhythm, visual imagery, melodic combinations, reverse structure, unusual adjectives/adverbs, sense of humor, philosophical bent (Piirto, 1999, p. 241).

Creative Area

The key characteristic that is often associated with creativity is *divergent thinking*. As opposed to convergent thinking (arriving at a single conclusion), divergent thinking requires the gifted and talented student to produce many ideas or ideas that are different from the norm.

Coleman and Cross (2001) suggest that the comparison group, "whether to self, others, a situation, a point in time, a field of study, a cultural group, or a combination of these," determines how narrowly or broadly creativity is defined (p. 241). Psychologists tend to agree that creativity is not the same as intelligence, but that creative individuals tend to have a threshold intelligence score of about 120 (Getzels & Jackson, 1962). Psychometrically, test developers have defined creativity as fluency, flexibility, originality, and elaboration (Guilford, 1950; Torrance, 1974). Cognitive scientists have identified characteristics of creative individuals by studying the methods they use in solving com-

9

plex problems (Perkins, 1981; Sternberg, 1988), while other researchers have identified characteristics by examining case studies of creators and how they generated ideas over longer periods of time (Goertzel & Goertzel, 1962; Gruber, 1982). Taking a case study approach, Gardner (1993) suggests that creative production emerges only after 10 years of concentrated study in a specific field. For this reason, teachers clearly would be observing creative potential in gifted and talented students during their school years.

Researchers have identified some of these common characteristics (Clark, 1997; Coleman & Cross, 2001; Gardner, 1993; Gilliam, Carpenter, & Christensen, 1996; Goertzel & Goertzel, 1962; Gruber, 1982; Guilford, 1950; Khatena, 1992; Perkins, 1981; Piirto, 1999; Renzulli, Smith, White, Callahan, Harman, & Westberg, 2002; Sternberg, 1988; Tannenbaum, 1983; Torrance, 1974):

- Has in-depth foundational knowledge.
- Prefers complexity and open-endedness.
- Contributes new concepts, methods, products, or performances.
- Has extreme fluency of thoughts and a large number of ideas.
- Is observant and pays attention to detail.
- Uses unique solutions to problems, improvises.
- Challenges existing ideas and products.
- Connects disparate ideas.
- Is constantly asking questions.
- Criticizes constructively.
- Is a risk taker, confident.
- Is attracted to the novel, complex, and mysterious.
- Is a nonconformist, uninhibited in expression, adventurous, able to resist group pressure.
- Accepts disorder.
- Tolerates ambiguity; delays closure.
- Is persistent and task committed in area of interest.
- Has a sense of humor.
- Is intellectually playful.
- Is aware of own creativity.
- Is emotionally sensitive; sensitive to beauty.
- Is intuitive.

- Enjoys alone time.
- Is reflective about personal creative process.

Artistic Area

In this area, gifted and talented students exhibit potential or demonstrated accomplishment in one or more artistic fields, such as art, drama, or music. Khatena (1992) suggested that "talented individuals in the performing and visual arts are bright, that creativity is a significant energizing factor in talent, and that specific to each art form exists highly specialized abilities that require the language and skills peculiar to that art form for their expression" (p. 147).

Researchers have identified general and specific characteristics for these artistic fields (Clark & Zimmerman, 1984; Gilliam, Carpenter, & Christensen, 1996; Renzulli, Smith, White, Callahan, & Harman, 1976; Khatena, 1988; 1992; Piirto, 1999; Seashore, Leavis, & Saetveit, 1960):

General (demonstrated within artistic area)

- Chooses artistic activity for projects or during free time.
- Studies or practices artistic talent without being told.
- Strives to improve artistic skills.
- Demonstrates talent for an extended period of time.
- Concentrates for long periods of time on artistic projects.
- Seems to pick up skills in the arts with little or no instruction.
- Possesses high sensory sensitivity.
- Observes and shows interest in others who are proficient in the artistic skill.
- Uses the artistic area to communicate.
- Experiments in the artistic medium.
- Sets high standards in the artistic area.
- Demonstrates confidence in the artistic area.

Art

- Scribbles earlier than most.
- Initiates drawing.

11

- Incorporates large number of elements into artwork.
- Provides balance and order in artwork.
- Elaborates on ideas from other people as a starting point.
- Observes details in environment, artistic area.
- Has unique, unusual solutions to artistic problems.
- Uses unusual and interesting visual imagery.
- Is innovative in selecting and using art materials.
- Has a highly developed sense of movement and rhythm in drawings.
- Has a great feel for color.
- Varies organization of elements to suit different situations.
- Uses content that is interesting, tells a story, or expresses feelings.
- Produces many drawings.

Drama

- Is innovative and creative in performing.
- Easily tells a story or gives an account of some experience.
- Uses gestures or facial expressions to communicate feelings.
- Is adept at role-playing, improvising, acting out situations.
- Identifies with moods and motivations of characters.
- Handles body with ease and poise.
- Creates original plays or makes up plays from stories.
- Commands and holds the attention of a group when speaking.
- Evokes emotional responses from listeners.
- Communicates feelings through nonverbal means.
- Imitates others, uses voice to reflect changes of idea and mood.

Music

12

- Discriminates fine differences in tone, relative, or absolute pitch.
- Identifies a variety of sounds (background noise, singers, orchestral instruments).

- Varies loudness and softness.
- Remembers melodies and can produce them accurately.
- Plays an instrument or indicates a strong desire.
- Is sensitive to rhythm, changes body movements to tempo.
- Dances to tunes with different rhythms.
- Can complete a melody.
- Creates own melodies.
- Likes listening to music.
- Likes producing music with others.

Leadership

Leadership is the result of an interaction between a number of variables: the personality, status, achievement, and intelligence of the leader; the characteristics of the followers; and the situation (Stogdill, 1974). Since leadership may emerge in various types of situations and is dependent upon a number of variables being present, professionals may find it difficult to identify potential leaders.

Knowing that the situation will influence leadership, researchers have identified these general personal characteristics (Davis & Rimm, 1994; Karnes, 1991; Khatena, 1992; Renzulli, Smith, White, Callahan, & Harman, 1976)

- Is well-organized.
- Can do backward planning.
- Is visionary, has a holistic view.
- Is a problem finder.
- Is able to see problems from multiple perspectives.
- Is adaptable to new situations.
- Can manipulate systems.
- Is highly responsible; can be counted on.
- Maintains on-task focus.
- Is self-confident.
- Is a persuasive communicator.
- Has a cooperative attitude; works well in groups.
- Participates in most social activities, enjoys being around other people.
- Influences the behavior of others; recognized as a leader by peers.

- Is respected, liked, or both by others.
- Is aware of verbal and nonverbal cues; sophisticated inter-personal skills.
- Is emotionally stable.
- Is willing to take risks.

Affective

Along with cognitive characteristics, gifted students frequently exhibit particular affective characteristics (Clark, 1997; Colangelo & Davis, 1991; Coleman & Cross, 2001; Khatena, 1992; Piirto, 1999; Rogers, 2001; Sternberg & Davidson, 1986; Swassing, 1985; Tannenbaum, 1983). Some researchers suggest that these emotional aspects of a gifted and talented individual may be traits or temperaments (i.e., genetic), while others may be developed (Csikszentmihalyi, Rathunde, & Whalen, 1993; Piirto, 1999; Winner, 1996):

- Is motivated in work that excites.
- Persists in completing tasks in areas of interest.
- Is self-directed, independent.
- Evaluates and judges critically.
- Has high degree of concentration.
- Becomes bored with routine tasks.
- Is interested in "adult" problems.
- Is concerned about right and wrong, ethics.
- Has higher self-concept, particularly in academics.
- Has high expectations of self and others.
- Has a sense of humor.
- Is highly sensitive.
- Takes other perspectives; is empathic.
- Is a perfectionist.

Characteristics of the Hard-to-Find Gifted and Talented Student

14

The interaction between these frequently cited characteristics associated with gifted and talented students and other factors such as the school task, the social situation, family background, and individual genetic traits can produce both desirable and undesirable behaviors (Clark, 1997; Whitmore, 1980). Undesirable behaviors tend to limit services for some gifted and talented students because teachers and other educators may have particular stereotypical expectations of how gifted students should perform (e.g., all are early readers, academic achievers, verbal, and "well-behaved students"). In Whitmore's classic study, she found certain factors that appear to influence underachievement in gifted students. This set of factors mainly falls within three categories: school conditions, motivation, and personal characteristics that may lead to problems (see Table 1.1).

When these factors are present, the gifted and talented student may not exhibit the characteristics that are listed in each of the above areas, but will choose to perform in school by rejecting assignments, functioning nonconstructively in groups, demonstrating poor study habits, procrastinating, showing a gap between oral and written work, or rebelling against teachers. Given these poor academic behaviors, the gifted and talented student may select companions who are negative toward school, alienate peers by constant aggression, or withdraw from social interactions in the classroom, at home, or both. These types of behaviors may ultimately lead to less satisfaction with school "rewards" such as grades or dropping out mentally or physically from school (Clark, 1997; Davis & Rimm, 1994; Laffoon, Jenkins-Friedman, & Tollefson, 1989; Whitmore, 1980).

Some groups of students are particularly vulnerable to exhibiting these negative behaviors or behaviors that are not necessarily stereotypical of gifted and talented students. These groups include culturally different students, those from lower income families, disabled students, and women.

Culturally Different

"Culturally different" refers frequently to gifted students from specific ethnic groups: Hispanics, African Americans, Native Americans, and Asian Americans. If the particular gifted student's "abilities and interests are not synchronous with subgroup values, then the child must face the problems of gaining acceptance of his or her giftedness by both society and by members of the subgroup" (p. 197). Areas of cultural identity are multifaceted and include not only national origin, but also religion, geographic region, urban/suburban/rural, age, gender/sex, class, and excep-

Table 1.1

Vulnerable Areas for Gifted Students

Personal Characteristics	Motivation	School Conditions
1. Perfectionism leads to high degree of self-criticism, competition, and/or unrealistic performance expectations.	1. Too easy or too difficult a task limits the GT student's possibility for success.	1. If individuality is not valued, then social isolation occurs.
2. Supersensitivity to social feedback leads to withdrawal.	2. The GT student fears failure from high expectations.	2. Teachers and others have unrealistic expectations of high performance in all areas consistently.
3. Desire for independence leads to attempts to control the situation.	3. Desires and abilities may not match opportunities.	3. Teachers and others are uncomfortable with differentness, fear superior knowledge.
4. Given an intense desire to satisfy curiosity, the GT student feels restricted in analyzing the problem in the time allocated.	4. No positive role model is present.	4. School activities are not differentiated or challenging, offer no depth or complexity.
5. Using advanced problem solving, the GT student manipulates peers and adults.	5. The GT student doesn't have a positive vision of the future.	5. The school district does not provide any appropriate educational provision.
6. Desiring complexity, the GT student is not interested in memorization, repetition, or lower levels of thinking.	6. The GT student doesn't have accurate self-knowledge about his ability.	
	7. Unable to control emotions, the GT student is easily frustrated, embarrassed, and aggressive toward people who create obstacles.	
	8. The GT student doesn't have the energy to persist to completion of a goal.	

Note. Adapted from *Giftedness, Conflict, and Underachievement*, by J. R. Whitmore, 1980, Boston: Allyn and Bacon. Copyright ©1980 by Allyn and Bacon. Adapted with permission.

tionality (Clark, 1997; Gollnick & Chinn, 1990). The greater number of areas that are different from the macro culture, the greater chance that the gifted student will display characteristics that may be different from the norm.

Torrance (1969) suggested 18 "creative positives" that may be helpful in identifying culturally different youth (pp. 71–81):

- ability to express feelings and emotions;
- ability to improvise with commonplace materials and objects;
- articulateness in role-playing, sociodrama, and story-telling;
- enjoyment of, and ability in, visual arts, such as drawing, painting, and sculpture;
- enjoyment of, and ability in, creative movement, dance, dramatics, and so forth;
- enjoyment of, and ability in, music, rhythm, and so forth;
- use of expressive speech;
- fluency and flexibility in figural media;
- enjoyment of, and skills in, small-group activities, problem solving, and so forth;
- responsiveness to the concrete;
- responsiveness to the kinesthetic;
- expressiveness of gestures, body language, and so forth, and ability to interpret body language;
- humor;
- richness of imagery in informal language;
- originality of ideas in problem solving;
- problem-centeredness or persistence in problem solving;
- emotional responsiveness; and
- quickness of warm-up.

On the other hand, Frasier and Passow (1994) suggested that all gifted students, regardless of their cultural background, express their abilities by demonstrating:

- a strong desire to learn;
- an intense, sometimes unusual interest;
- an unusual ability to communicate with words, numbers, or symbols;

17

- effective, often inventive strategies for recognizing and solving problems;
- a large storehouse of information;
- a quick grasp of new concepts;
- logical approaches to solutions;
- many highly original ideas; and
- an unusual sense of humor.

Lower Income

Children from lower income backgrounds have the most difficulty in being selected for programs for gifted and talented students (Clark, 1997). They may have a family background that is not rich in language and reading or family members who have not had positive experiences with school, who have not attained higher education degrees, or who solve problems using violence (Baldwin, 1973). For these reasons, this group of gifted students is particularly vulnerable to becoming underachievers in school.

Researchers have identified these characteristics that appear to assist in identifying children from lower income backgrounds (Baldwin, 1973; Clark, 1997; Torrance, 1969):

- Has high mathematical abilities.
- Is curious; varied interests.
- Is independent.
- Has a good imagination.
- Is fluent in nonverbal communication.
- Improvises when solving problems.
- Learns quickly through experience.
- Retains and uses information well.
- Shows a desire to learn in daily work.
- Is original and creative.
- Uses language rich in imagery.
- Responds well to visual media; concrete activities.
- Shows leadership among peers; is responsible.
- Shows relationships among unrelated ideas.
- Is entrepreneurial.
- Has a keen sense of humor.

Disabled

It has been estimated that approximately 2% of the disabled population is gifted. Children with disabilities include those with learning disabilities, visual or auditory impairments, physical disabilities, emotional handicaps, or speech delays. Most often, the child may have extreme ability in one or more areas and need remediation in others. The disability may mask the ability or vice versa. For example, a gifted child with a hearing impairment may be delayed in language and may need assistance from a speech therapist. Since special education services often focus on remediation, the gift might go unrecognized. On the other hand, a gifted child with a learning disability may be able to answer comprehension questions on a test by matching words in the passage to the answers even though she doesn't know how to read. In this case, the gifted student would hide the disability and most likely not be served by special education or the program for gifted and talented students.

Table 1.2 includes the characteristics Whitmore (1981) has identified that reveal giftedness in children with disabilities.

Women

For the most part, boys and girls do not differ significantly in cognitive skills (Kerr, 1991; Linn & Hyde, 1989; Maccoby & Jacklin, 1974). In fact, gifted girls are more similar to gifted boys than to average girls in their interests, attitudes, and aspirations (Kerr, 1991). However, while changing, the culture still tends to encourage more passivity in girls (e.g., playing with dolls, reading) and more spatial and analytic reasoning in boys (e.g., playing video games, using building blocks; Clark, 1997). Girls who show talent may be viewed as unfeminine, bossy, and show-offs, thus more girls hide their talents by adolescence. Teachers need to be particularly diligent in identifying girls for programs in mathematics and science. Kitano (1994/1995) and Kerr (1994) suggested that research on mainstream gifted women may not necessarily generalize to gifted women from other ethnic and racial groups.

twice exceptional

Table 1.2

Characteristics of Gifted and Disabled Students

Disability	Impeding Characteristics	Characteristics Revealing Giftedness
Learning disability	Little or no productivity in school—cannot read, write, spell easily or accurately	1. Superiority in oral language—vocabulary, fluency, structure 2. Memory for facts and events 3. Exceptional comprehension 4. Analytical and creative problem-solving abilities 5. Markedly advanced interests, impressive knowledge 6. Keen perception and humor 7. Superior memory, general knowledge
Developmental delay in motor area	Poor motor skills, coordination. Writing is painfully slow, messy. Child is often easily distracted from tasks and described as inattentive.	1. Drive to communicate through alternative modes: visual, nonverbal body language. 2. Superior memory and problem-solving ability 3. Exceptional interest and drive in response to challenge
Cerebral palsy, deafness	Absence of oral communication skills.	1. Superior verbal skill, oral language 2. Exceptional capacity for manipulating people and solving "problems" 3. Superior memory, general knowledge
Emotional handicap	Disordered behavior—aggressive, disruptive, frequently off-task. Extremely withdrawn, noncommunicative.	Most difficult to identify—the only key is response to stimulation of higher mental abilities unless superior written work is produced.

Note. Adapted from "Gifted Children With Handicapping Conditions: A New Frontier," by J. R. Whitmore, 1981, *Exceptional Children, 2,* p. 106. Copyright ©1981 by the Council for Exceptional Children.

Summary

Gifted and talented students present an array of characteristics in one or more of the areas defined in federal and state definitions. These characteristics may be manifested in both positive and negative ways. In all cases, teachers must provide opportunities for the characteristic to be demonstrated. Directors and coordinators of school districts must provide professional development so that teachers will know how to establish situations for gifts and talents to emerge, how to observe characteristics over time, and how to observe characteristics in groups that are typically underrepresented in programs for gifted and talented students (culturally different, lower income, disabled, and women).

CHAPTER TWO

Qualitative and Quantitative Approaches to Assessment

by Gail R. Ryser

The Texas State Plan for the Education of Gifted/Talented Students (Texas Education Agency, 1996) includes 10 guidelines in the area of student assessment. One of these is: "Assessment in the areas of intellectual and specific academic fields, grades 1–12, uses a minimum of three (3) appropriate criteria that include both qualitative and quantitative measures" (p. 9). As this guideline illustrates, a district must use at least three criteria that include both qualitative and quantitative measures. These measures should match the district program and have adequate reliability and validity.

The focus of this chapter is on qualitative and quantitative approaches to assessment and how district personnel can choose sound measures of both types. Before professionals can choose measures that are both qualitative and quantitative, they must have a clear conceptual understanding of what these terms mean. The next section provides definitions of both.

Definition of Qualitative and Quantitative Measures

According to *Webster's II New College Dictionary* (Houghton Mifflin, 1995), qualitative means "of, relating to, or concerning quality" (p. 905) and quantitative means "expressed or capable of expression as a quantity" (p. 905). Assessments that are considered qualitative use *words to describe* and understand an individual's strengths or other characteristics, while quantitative assessments use *numbers to describe* and understand an individual's strengths or other characteristics.

A second distinction between the two approaches is the degree to which the assessment is dynamic. Qualitative measures provide flexibility to the examiner and the examinee, whereas quantitative measures provide a blueprint to be followed. For example, in portfolio assessment, there is usually some *freedom* for the examinee to decide on the contents of the portfolio. Quantitative assessments, on the other hand, are much more *controlled,* and change is considered undesirable.

A third distinction is the degree to which the assessment task simulates performance in the real world. Qualitative assessments can be of two types. Restricted performance tasks consist of more structured tasks that are limited in scope, such as writing on a given topic. Extended performance tasks are more comprehensive and less structured, such as writing a short story on a self-selected topic. Quantitative assessments typically consist of selected response tasks, in which the examinee chooses the correct or best answer in a multiple-choice, true/false, or matching format, or supply response tasks, in which the examinee responds with a word, short phrase, or short written essay. On one end of the continuum are the selected response quantitative assessments that are low in realism since such highly structured problems seldom occur in real life. Extended performance assessments are high in realism since they try to simulate performance in the real world (Gronlund, 1998).

Too often, examiners gather information using qualitative assessments, but use the results quantitatively. For example, a portfolio of student work might be judged holistically and provided a single score. If the single score is the only information provided to the identification committee, the portfolio, in effect, is a quantitative measure. To be truly qualitative, the rich description one can glean from the portfolio should be included in the committee's decision-making process. In Chapter 5, we provide examples of how a district can combine qualitative and quantitative information to make better decisions about each student's strengths. It is important to include both types of assessment when identifying students as gifted and talented since the combination provides a more complete description and better understanding of their strengths.

Types of Qualitative Assessments

This section describes three types of qualitative assessments most commonly used to identify students as gifted. These are portfolios, interviews, and observations.

Portfolios

A portfolio is a purposeful collection of student work that exhibits progress in a particular area (Arter, 1990). Advantages to using portfolio assessment in identifying gifted students are that they:

- focus on the positive,
- include samples of best performance, and
- include reflections of student work over time.

While evidence suggests that portfolios can be useful in predicting students' success in programs designed for gifted students (Johnsen & Ryser, 1997), there are some problems associated with their use. One of the most pressing problems is understanding the procedures used in collecting student work. For example, teachers may think that the portfolio is simply a folder of work that the student has completed in the classroom. Instead, it is a collection of products and performances that might be collected at home, at school, or both to demonstrate a specific set of student characteristics (e.g., creative writing, mathematics ability, the visual arts, etc.). Johnsen and Ryser found that, when students and teachers are taught what a portfolio is, what should be included, and how to collect the items; the final portfolio is of higher quality. The work that is collected in the portfolio should be both teacher-generated (i.e., all students include the same type of product) and student-generated (i.e., each student may include different types of products). Each item should also contain student reflection. For example, the

25

student might write or dictate, "I included this mathematics worksheet in my portfolio because it shows that I am doing math at a higher grade level."

Two related problems are developing sound criteria used to judge the merits of the portfolio and training scorers to use these criteria. Criteria should be predetermined and may be either holistic (e.g., the criterion is present or not present) or based on a Likert-type scale (e.g., 1 = never to 5 = frequently). Evans (1993) suggested that educators work collaboratively to produce clear descriptions of criteria and use existing collections of student work. For example, the Texas Student Portfolio (Texas Education Agency, n.d..) uses the following criteria for judging products and performances:

- details in presentation of an idea;
- creative responses to tasks;
- work advanced beyond grade level;
- in-depth understanding of an idea, skill, or subject;
- evidence of leadership skills;
- vocabulary advanced beyond age or grade level;
- keen sense of humor; and
- high-quality work.

Student work that shows promise would be placed into a high group, work that is average would be placed into a medium group, and work that is inadequate would be placed into a low group. Using these groups, educators could develop a specific list of characteristics and models for each point on a qualitative scale. For example, the Lubbock Independent School District (Shambeck, Duncan, & Dougherty, 1988) presented these examples of ways in which gifted and talented students might exhibit "details in presentation of an idea":

- Art (primary): Jesse always elaborates on his drawings. He adds countless details to his pictures. When drawing a person, he puts patterns in the clothing, laces and eyelets on the shoes, fingernails, and so forth.
- Art (intermediate). Jesse always elaborates on his drawings. His drawings and paintings are filled with both line and color detail that adds to the impact of this work.
- Oral language (primary): Wyatt is the class storyteller.

When sharing an experience with the class, he adds countless details to his story, describing everything to the *nth* degree.

- Oral language (intermediate). Wyatt exhibits a great talent for public speaking. His class oral reports are filled with elaboration. He describes everything to the *nth* degree, adding countless informative details. He doesn't even need notes.

In summary, portfolios provide qualitative information that provides evidence of characteristics in specific domains. Professional development is needed so that students and teachers understand the purpose of the portfolio, what evidence might be included in a portfolio, how to collect the items, and how to evaluate using specific criteria.

Interviews

A second type of qualitative assessment approach is the interview. Interviews have widespread use in clinical diagnosis and counseling, but only recently have they been used in the identification of gifted students. While many professionals advocate using interviews, little research can be found about how interviews fare in the identification of gifted students. In spite of the lack of research, interviews hold promise in the field for identifying students as gifted, especially those from low-income or culturally diverse backgrounds.

Interviews can be either structured or unstructured. In a structured interview, the interviewer asks each respondent a set of preestablished questions with a limited set of responses (Denzin & Lincoln, 1994). In this situation, all respondents receive the same questions in the same order. This type of interview is designed to capture precise data in order to explain behavior in preestablished categories. Unstructured interviews are open ended; interviewers may have some general topics to broach, but not a specific set of questions or a limited set of response choices.

For example, Pulaski County Special School District in Little Rock, AR, has used interviews at both the elementary and secondary levels to identify students for their Alpha Classes

27

(Anthony, 1989). The interviews have both structured and unstructured questions. Below is a structured question at the elementary level

1. Suppose you were studying the solar system in science. If your teacher gave you a choice of three assignments (assuming all three were worth the same number of points), which one would you choose?
    a. Look up planets in the encyclopedia. Write one fact about each of the nine planets. Use your best handwriting and turn in your work.
    b. Choose two planets. Write a paragraph describing life on each one. Give a speech to the class explaining why one would be the best place for the human colony.
    c. Build a model of the solar system that lights up and rotates. (p. 30)

An example of an unstructured question at the secondary level is: "Do you or did you ever have a collection? What do you collect? How did you get started on your collection?" (p. 63).

At the elementary level, the interviews are scored using three characteristics: learning, motivation, and creativity (Anthony, 1989). For example, in the above structured interview item, response "b" would be scored as showing evidence of learning and motivation, whereas response "c" would be scored as showing evidence of motivation and creativity (p. 33). At the secondary level, the program facilitators are encouraged to use questioning that might reveal problem-solving abilities that would not normally be observed by the classroom teacher. The director of the gifted program suggests that the questions are merely to be used as examples of types of questions that might be asked. "The facilitator should feel free to design questions during the process of the interview in order to more completely identify characteristics and interests reflective of this particular student" (p. 63).

In summary, interviews should be a combination of structured and unstructured questions. Some questions should be asked of all students, but the response set should not be limited. Interviewers should also have the freedom to probe and clarify responses.

Observations

Observations are made with the intention of finding students who demonstrate gifted characteristics at school, at home, or in other settings. Observers should have an opportunity to observe the child in situations where the child can demonstrate his or her potential. This often necessitates the need to go beyond the classroom walls and use not only teachers, but parents, peers, and other community members.

Observations can be made using a rating scale, checklist, "jot down" procedure, or nomination form of gifted characteristics. Rating scales are generally more quantitative than other types of observations, and characteristics are usually rated using a Likert scale.

Norm-Referenced Rating Scales

There are several rating scales for recording observations of gifted behaviors. Two examples of norm-referenced rating scales are the Scales for Identifying Gifted Students (SIGS; Ryser & McConnell, 2004) and the Gifted and Talented Evaluation Scales (GATES; Gilliam, Carpenter, & Christensen, 1996).

The SIGS can be used to rate a child's strengths in seven areas: general intellectual ability, language arts, mathematics, science, social studies, creativity, and leadership. The SIGS has two forms: a School Rating Scale (SRS) and a Home Rating Scale (HRS). The HRS is also available in Spanish. Educators and parents or caregivers rate a student's strengths using a 0–4-point Likert scale. The higher the point value on the scale, the more the child demonstrates the characteristic when compared to age peers. The SIGS is appropriate for children and adolescents ages 5–18.

The GATES can be used to rate student's strengths in five areas: intellectual ability, academic skills, creativity, leadership, and artistic talent. It uses a 9-point Likert scale and consists of one form that can be completed by teachers or parents. The GATES is appropriate for children and adolescents ages 5 through 18.

Because these are norm-referenced, a standard score for each scale can be derived. Sometimes, parents and teachers may not discriminate among the behaviors, but will rate all behaviors using

29

the highest score possible. This may render the rating scale invalid for identifying students as gifted. A strategy many educators use to make sure that each characteristic is being considered in relationship to the student is to ask teachers or parents for examples. These examples can be provided in writing or in an interview. It is important to simplify the process so that teachers and parents are able to share their observations.

Other Observation Tools

Sometimes, teachers have difficulty remembering sets of characteristics that students have exhibited over a period of time and find a "jot down" approach more helpful (Texas Education Agency, n.d.). With a "jot down," a teacher records the observed characteristic as it occurs in the classroom. For example, Figure 2.1 shows a "jot down" for identifying students in the language arts area that uses characteristics from the Feldhusen, Hoover, and Sayler (1990) checklists at the secondary level.

Peers are also helpful in observing their friend's behaviors. They sometimes know more about a student than teachers do or parents do. Gagné, Bégin, and Talbot (1993) created a peer nomination form that encourages peers to nominate friends who exhibit characteristics in a variety of talent areas that they label with creative, yet descriptive names such as "encyclopedia," "confidant," "lightning," and so on. "Encyclopedia" is a girl or a boy who knows lots of things about all kinds of subjects, not just school subjects; a "confidant" is a girl or a boy who knows how to listen and does not repeat secrets that she or he receives. A confidant knows how to comfort other kids and make them feel better again; and a "lightning" is a girl or a boy who understands explanations quickly and often finds the right answers before the others (p. 41).

Finally, parents are helpful in identifying behaviors in the home that might not be exhibited at school. In fact, parents are actually better at identifying very young children (e.g., 76%) than teachers (4.3%) when using an intelligence test as the criterion (Jacobs, 1971). It's important to remember that parent forms should not be difficult to use, require writing abilities and numerous examples, or use educational jargon. Parents from lower income groups may not have the time, the system "wiseness," or the writing ability to complete complicated forms.

When a student shows evidence of the characteristics,
write his or her name in the matching box.
Place a tally mark by the name for each observation.

Extensive Vocabulary	Observant	Organizes Ideas
Sense of Humor	Reads Widely	Original and Creative
Writes independently	Likes Research	Point of View
Curious	Elaborates	Visualizes Images

Figure 2.1 Identification Jot Down

In summary, observations are important in identifying characteristics in a variety of settings. Again, professionals and others who are collecting examples should be trained in using norm-referenced scales or other observation tools. It's particularly important that parents understand validity issues and the problems that may arise for students when they are placed in programs that do not match their needs.

Types of Quantitative Measures

Two types of quantitative measures are norm-referenced and criterion-referenced measures. Norm-referenced measures compare an individual's score to others who also took the test. This comparison group is known as the normative sample. Criterion-referenced measures compare a person's performance to a specified content domain or external criterion. For example, a person's score may be compared to a level of mastery in a particular subject area. Because mastery levels are typically set at an average level, criterion-referenced measures are not usually recommended for identifying students as gifted. Therefore, this section discusses several types of norm-referenced measures: achievement, aptitude, and intelligence tests.

Achievement Tests

Achievement tests are designed to measure the effects of instruction (Anastasi & Urbina, 1997). In other words, achievement tests measure what an individual already knows or understands about a content area, such as mathematics. There are two issues a school district must consider when using achievement tests for identifying students as gifted. First, most achievement tests do not contain enough ceiling. Second, children enter school with varying amounts of acquired knowledge.

Ceiling effects. Stanley (1976) stated that most achievement tests used to identify students as gifted were inappropriate because they failed to have enough ceiling. This means that the test does not contain enough difficult items. Tests that are grade- or age-level calibrated are usually too easy for gifted students. Testing a student's limits can only be accomplished when a test is difficult enough to determine the extent of his or her knowledge. If a test is not difficult enough, two students scoring at the 99th percentile rank may actually have very different levels of knowledge and expertise in the content area being measured.

Two methods can be used to compensate for inadequate ceilings. First, many school districts use off-level aptitude and achievement measures to identify students as gifted. Off-level testing means that students are assessed using a version of a test intended for students who are older. For example, Stanley (1991) used the Scholastic Assessment Test–Mathematics (SAT-M; Educational Testing Service, 1989) with students who were much younger than those for whom the test was developed. Students scoring from 500–800 on the SAT-M were then selected to participate in a program for mathematically precocious youth.

A second strategy is to use norm-referenced achievement tests that were developed specifically to identify students as gifted. Two such measures are the Screening Assessment for Gifted Elementary and Middle School Students–Second Edition (SAGES-2; Johnsen & Corn, 2001) and the Test of

Mathematical Abilities for Gifted Students (TOMAGS; Ryser & Johnsen, 1998).

The SAGES-2 (Johnsen & Corn, 2001) has three subtests, two of which measure achievement in mathematics/science and language arts/social studies. The third subtest is a nonverbal reasoning measure. The SAGES-2 is appropriate for students ages 5–14. Because the test was developed for and with gifted students, it has enough ceiling and will differentiate among gifted students. The SAGES-2 is also developmentally appropriate for young students. Items for younger students (ages 5–9) are read aloud so reading ability does not interfere with the outcome. In addition, these students record their answers on the test booklet by drawing a vertical line through their response choice. Students are taught how to mark their responses before taking the test.

The TOMAGS (Ryser & Johnsen, 1998) was developed to identify students who are gifted in mathematics. It can be used to test students ages 6–12. The TOMAGS uses a mathematical problem-solving and reasoning approach to measure mathematical talent. Items on the TOMAGS can be read aloud to students who then record their responses directly on the test booklet.

Acquired knowledge. A second consideration with using achievement tests to identify students as gifted is the varying levels of acquired knowledge and environmental enrichment of young children. Children from economically disadvantaged backgrounds sometimes have not been exposed to the types of experiences that go into acquired knowledge. Using an achievement test as a gatekeeper for entrance into a gifted program will almost always guarantee the underrepresentation of economically disadvantaged students in these programs.

School districts can compensate for these varying levels of acquired knowledge. First, achievement tests should *never* be used as the single criterion to move students to the screening phase when considering who should be placed in a gifted program. For example, a school district that only considers students who score at or above the 90th percentile rank on an achievement test for their gifted program is using this practice. Rather, school districts will want to use multiple sources during the nomination phase. Achievement scores could be one source, but never the sole source.

Second, school districts with large numbers of students from economically disadvantaged backgrounds may want to consider using achievement tests only to make decisions about placement in a particular academic program, not as a criterion for selection into the gifted program. As students progress through school, acquired knowledge becomes less of an issue, especially if students are placed in classes that meet their educational needs.

Aptitude and Intelligence Tests

Achievement, aptitude, and intelligence tests all sample aptitude, learning, and achievement to some degree (Sattler, 2001). The difference lies in the specificity of the content and the link they have to formal learning in school or at home. Both aptitude and intelligence testing are not as domain-specific as achievement tests. Therefore, we discuss these two types of norm referenced measures together.

Aptitude tests are used to predict subsequent performance in a domain. Perhaps the most well known example of what we define as an aptitude test is the Scholastic Assessment Test (SAT; Educational Testing Service, 1989), which is widely used for entrance into colleges because it is said to be a good predictor of college performance. In addition, off-level SAT testing is sometimes used to enter students into specific academic programs for the gifted (see discussion above).

Intelligence testing has engendered much controversy in the area of assessment. This controversy stems from a basic misunderstanding about what intelligence tests measure. Intelligence tests do not measure innate ability; rather, they sample behaviors already learned in an attempt to predict future learning (McLouglin & Lewis, 2001). Most intelligence tests do this by measuring a person's ability to apply information in new and different ways.

The biggest consideration for districts when using aptitude or intelligence tests to identify students as gifted is the degree to which they are useful in identifying students from culturally and linguistically diverse backgrounds. Districts with high numbers of these students must determine the level of verbal content included in a particular test being considered as an identification tool. Districts using a test that is high in verbal content will likely iden-

34

tify fewer students from culturally or linguistically diverse backgrounds.

An example of an intelligence test with high verbal content is the Slosson Intelligence Tests–Revised (SIT-R; Slosson, Nicholson, & Hibpshman, 1998). The SIT-R consists of 187 items that are read aloud to the examinee. The items encompass memory, vocabulary, general information, similarities and differences, comprehension, and quantitative problems. Because this test is heavily loaded with verbal content, it should not be used with speakers of other languages and should be used with caution with students from culturally and linguistically diverse backgrounds.

Alternatives to tests that have high verbal content are nonverbal tests. To be truly nonverbal, a test must eliminate the role of language in the content, administration, and response requirements. Researchers have found nonverbal aptitude and intelligence tests promising for the identification of gifted students from culturally and linguistically diverse backgrounds (Naglieri & Ford, 2003; Zurcher, 1998). Examples of nonverbal tests include the Test of Nonverbal Intelligence–Third Edition (TONI-3; Brown, Sherbenou, & Johnsen, 1997), the Comprehensive Test of Nonverbal Intelligence (C-TONI; Hammill, Pearson, & Wiederholt, 1997), and the Naglieri Nonverbal Ability Test (NNAT; Naglieri, 2003).

The TONI-3 (Brown, Sherbenou, & Johnsen, 1997) provides pantomime or spoken directions so the test can be administered completely language-free. It consists of two forms of 45 items each and takes approximately 15–20 minutes to administer. Items are abstract/figural in content and present the examinee with a novel problem. For example, an examinee will look at a pattern and choose the best answer from six response choices. The TONI-3 provides the examiner with one score, a Nonverbal Intelligence Quotient.

The C-TONI (Hammill, Pearson, & Wiederholt, 1997) also provides pantomime or spoken directions. The test measures analogical reasoning, categorical classification, and sequential reasoning in two different contexts: pictures and geometric designs. Examinees look at a group of picture or designs and solve problems involving analogies, categorizations, and sequences. The C-TONI provides three scores: an overall Nonverbal Intelligence Quotient, a

Pictorial Nonverbal Intelligence Quotient, and a Geometric Nonverbal Intelligence Quotient.

The NNAT (Naglieri, 1997) is a brief nonverbal measure comprised of progressive matrix items using shapes and geometric designs. The shapes and designs are interrelated through spatial or logical organization. Students are required to examine relationships among the parts of the matrix and choose the response that best completes it. The NNAT provides one score, a Nonverbal Ability Index.

Reliability Issues in Assessment

According to the *Standards for Educational and Psychological Testing* (American Educational Research Association, American Psychological Association, & National Council on Measurement in Education, 1999), reliability refers to the consistency of measurement "when the testing procedure is repeated on a population of individuals or groups" (p. 25). Reliability is the difference between a person's observed outcome and true outcome in an assessment. This difference is measurement error, the random or unpredictable fluctuations that can occur in assessment outcomes. Error occurs in all types of measurement. For example, a clock measures time. If the clock displays a different time from the true time (i.e., the clock is running slow or running fast), the clock has measurement error. Fluctuations on tests occur as a result of the examinee or other factors that are external to the examinee. Sources of error that can be attributed to the examinee are factors such as motivation, anxiety, and attention. Factors external to the examinee include testing conditions and examiner competence.

Assessments that use standardized administration procedures and test formats will likely have less error in measurement than those with greater flexibility in these areas. Therefore, quantitative assessments are typically more reliable because they are less flexible than qualitative assessments. For example, portfolios of student work allow a wide choice of formats (e.g., videos, to model prototypes, to written essays). On the other hand, this flexibility may mean that the outcome is more reflective of an individual's strengths.

Error in measurement reduces the degree to which the results can be generalized. According to Anastasi and Urbina (1997), there are three sources of error that can occur in assessments:

- content—the degree to which the content or items on the assessment are measuring the same construct;
- time—the extent to which the outcome of the test will be the same when it is administered at different times; and
- interscorer—how well two examiners will score the results the same.

All three sources of error are found in both qualitative and quantitative assessments. Regardless of which approach one takes, both are evaluated using the same set of standards. The manner in which one reports them, however, and the questions asked will differ. Table 2.1 illustrates the three sources of errors and the questions an examiner would want to answer about each source as it relates to qualitative or quantitative assessments.

Validity Issues in Assessment

Validity is the "degree to which evidence and theory support the interpretation of test scores" (American Educational Research Association, American Psychological Association, & National Council on Measurement in Education, 1999, p. 9). At the heart of validity is how closely a test's outcome matches with what the examiner is trying to measure. Two issues that affect the validity of a measure are construct underrepresentation and construct irrelevance. Construct underrepresentation occurs when the domain sampled does not adequately represent the construct under consideration. For a mathematics achievement test, construct underrepresentation would occur if the test consisted only of computation problems. Construct irrelevance is the degree to which test scores are influenced by other variables that are not part of the construct being measured. Construct irrelevance would occur if reading level interfered with an individual's ability to answer questions on a mathematics achievement test.

According to the *Standards for Education and Psychological Testing* (American Educational Research Association, American

37

Table 2.1

Questions Regarding the Three Sources of Error Related to Reliability in Qualitative and Quantitative Assessments

Type of reliability	Qualitative	Quantitative
Content	Is the sample of work consistent with other samples of the same student's work? Are the characteristics or interview questions that are measuring the same construct related to one another? Is there consistency in the way the samples of work are collected, the observations made and the interview questions asked?	Do all items on a subtest correlate with one another? Is there evidence that assessments with alternate forms are equivalent? Are the standard errors of measurement reasonable and are they reported? Is there evidence that the test is equally reliable for different gender or ethnic groups?
Time	Do the samples of work collected, the characteristics observed, or answers to interview questions differ dramatically depending on the time period in which the assessment was made (not as a result of intervention or maturation)? Are there variables that would interfere with the collection of samples of work, characteristics observed, or answers to interview questions at different times?	Do the test-retest studies show that a person's test performance is stable over time (taking into account changes due to maturation or intervention)? Is this evidence provided for all ages for which the test is applicable? For tests with alternate forms, are test-retest studies reported showing the stability of Form 1 to Form 2?
Interscorer	Are the scorers consistent in their evaluation of the assessment outcomes? To what degree have the scorers been trained? Would different observers agree on the presence or absence of a given characteristic? Would different interviewers obtain the same responses from the same student?	Is the test set up in a way to minimize scorer errors? Is there evidence that examiners are consistent in their scoring? When an examiner has to make more subjective decisions, would different examiners be consistent?

Table 2.2

Questions Regarding Three Types of Validity Evidence Related to Reliability in Qualitative and Quantitative Assessments

Type of reliability	Qualitative	Quantitative
Content-description	Is the sample of work, questions asked, and characteristics observed an adequate representative of the student's talent area?	Is a table of specifications developed that adequately illustrates the relationship of the items to the construct being measured?
Criterion-prediction	Is there evidence that the samples of work collected, the questions asked, and characteristics observed relate to what we are trying to measure or to future performance in the domain being measured?	Is there evidence that illustrates the relationship between the test and other measures of the same construct or future performance in the domain being measured?
Construct-identification	Can the sample of work, the responses to interview questions, or the characteristics observed be generalized to other situations?	Is there a body of evidence (e.g., factor analysis, convergent and discriminant validity) that shows that the test actually measures the hypothesized construct?

Psychological Association, & National Council on Measurement in Education, 1999), validity is the responsibility of both the test developer and the test user. The test developer must clearly delineate and provide evidence of how the results can be interpreted. Using our mathematics achievement measure as an example, the test developer would want to provide evidence that the test discriminates between students who do well in mathematics classes and those who do poorly. The test user is responsible for evaluating the validity information and for using and interpreting the results in ways that are supported by the validity evidence.

Anastasi and Urbina (1997) have defined three types of validity:

- content-description—the degree to which the test content covers a representative sample of the behavior that is being measured;
- criterion-prediction—the effectiveness with which the test predicts a person's performance in the specified activities measured by the test; and
- construct-identification—the extent to which the test measures what it purports to measure.

All three types of validity evidence should be reported for both qualitative and quantitative assessments. Table 2.2 illustrates the three types of validity evidence and the questions an examiner would want to answer about each as it relates to qualitative or quantitative assessments.

Summary

In summary, qualitative and quantitative approaches to assessment differ in how the results are recorded, the flexibility of the administration and content, and the degree to which the assessment matches realism. Using both approaches provides a more complete picture of an individual's strengths. While there are many types of qualitative and quantitative measures, examiners must consider reliability and validity for both.

CHAPTER THREE

Culture-Fair and Nonbiased Assessment

by Gail R. Ryser

T est fairness is an ethical issue for all individuals who develop and use measures to identify students as gifted. This is particularly important in view of one of the more persistent problems in the field of gifted education, namely the identification and provision of services for economically disadvantaged and culturally/linguistically diverse gifted students. Ford (1996) estimated that African American, Hispanic American, and Native American students were underrepresented by about 50% in programs for the gifted. This underrepresentation of minorities is particularly significant among those from lower income families.

Various explanations have been given for the underrepresentation of economically disadvantaged and culturally/linguistically diverse students in gifted programs. Some professionals feel that the problem lies in negative attitudes teachers and other educators hold about these students (Frasier, 1987). For example, teachers and other professionals may view these students as coming from environments that are limited in exposure to the types of experiences that go into intellectual development. Others believe that the nature of definitions and programs for the gifted create possible barriers. Many professionals in the field of gifted education view giftedness as a complex and multifaceted phenomenon that requires multiple sources of information for identification. Unfortunately, some school districts use only measures that are related primarily to school achievement, such as teacher nom-

41

inations and achievement tests. In other words, it is students who are high achievers that tend to be selected for gifted programs, rather than students with limited experiences who may not achieve as high, but who have high potential. Other researchers have examined whether disparity in test performance is a result of cultural differences. Fairness in standardized tests has been questioned in terms of the norms used for test interpretation, the language demands of the test items, possible item bias, and the purpose for which the test results are used.

In summary, a major issue in the field is providing services for economically disadvantaged and culturally/linguistically diverse gifted students. Barriers that exclude these students from programs for the gifted include (a) negative attitudes toward minority youngsters, particularly those from lower income backgrounds; (b) exclusive definitions that include only students with demonstrated high achievement; and (c) tests that are not fair for economically disadvantaged and culturally/linguistically diverse gifted students. The rest of this chapter will present strategies that can be used to overcome these barriers.

Negative Attitudes

Teachers and other educators who hold negative attitudes about the academic capabilities of culturally and linguistically diverse students, particularly those from economically disadvantaged backgrounds, generally have low academic expectations for them. For example, during the summers of 1987 and 1988, the University of Texas hosted an Institute for Young Disadvantaged Gifted Children (Johnsen & Ryser, 1994). The summer institute was designed to identify and provide services to young gifted children, ages 4–7, from economically disadvantaged backgrounds. Teachers in nine Chapter I-designated schools were asked to nominate students for the program. Prior to the nomination phase, teachers participated in a training session. As one teacher in this session stated, "There are no gifted children at this school. They all need remediation" (p. 62). This attitude promotes a deficit approach to these students' education, which makes the recognition of strengths difficult. In addition, taking a deficit approach to education detracts from creating needed changes in schools.

To overcome negative attitudes about the inclusion of these students in gifted programs and to promote change, effective advocacy is necessary. Grantham (2003) described the following four phases of an advocacy plan that resulted in an increase in the number of minority students in gifted programs in a school district in Arkansas: needs assessments, development of an advocacy plan, implementation, and follow-up and evaluation.

The needs assessment phase is designed to understand what is going on and what needs to happen. During this phase, effective advocates will gain an understanding of local- and state-level involvement in gifted education, identify target groups that can influence gifted programs and services, and define supporters and nonsupporters. During the development phase, participants are solicited, priorities are established, short-term and long-term goals are developed, and supporters are identified. The implementation phase is where informal and formal actions are taken. These should be in writing and have clearly defined outcomes. During the final phase, follow-up and evaluation, those involved reflect on the advocacy and establish direction for future efforts. The school district in this case study was under a federal court order to increase the number of African American students identified for the district's gifted and talented program. Other school districts struggling with underrepresentation of economically disadvantaged and culturally/linguistically diverse gifted students should take a proactive, rather than reactive, approach.

Robinson and Moon (2003) studied six exemplary local and state advocacy efforts in gifted education. They described four strategies that make advocacy efforts effective: planning, collaboration, communication, and program development. Most planning efforts took the form of lobbying and consensus building, although some planning focused on accomplishing specific outcomes. Robinson and Moon stated that, whatever form planning takes, it must fit the personality of the individuals involved in the advocacy effort. Collaboration was characterized by the development of conditions designed to influence decision makers. Because advocacy efforts can be adversarial in nature, collaboration was seen as a crucial strategy for winning the support needed to bring about change. The third strategy, communication, took three forms: raising awareness, discussing issues, and lobbying. Program development, the fourth strategy, was present in only two of the six advocacy efforts. These two made changes in programming for the purpose of creating change. For the other four advocacy efforts, change in program development was a result of the advocacy effort, rather than an advocacy strategy.

In summary, advocacy is important to promote change in teachers' and other professionals' attitudes and knowledge of culturally/linguistically diverse students, particularly those from lower income backgrounds. Advocacy efforts need to focus on helping teachers recognize indicators of potential in these students and provide opportunities for them to show their strengths.

Exclusive Definitions

In many states, a narrow definition of giftedness is used that is often limited to intelligence and academic achievement. States with narrow definitions that focus on intelligence and achievement typically use a psychometric approach to identify students as gifted. In fact, several states require that a student score two or more standard deviations above the mean (i.e., 130) on an individually administered intelligence test to be considered for selection in a gifted program.

The Texas definition for gifted and talented recognizes several areas in which performance may be exhibited (i.e., intellectual, creative, artistic, leadership, academic). Texas also requires that multiple criteria from multiple sources be used in the identification of gifted students. This is in line with current thinking and research in the field, which recognizes that intelligence takes many forms and that students' talents can be expressed in a myriad of ways.

Frasier (1997) has promoted the concept of using multiple criteria, that is, the gathering of comprehensive information about students' strengths from a variety of sources. Information gathered should be both quantitative and qualitative. In addition, it is important that educators not make decisions about providing services to students until all of the information can be reviewed. One practical problem in using multiple criteria is how to manage the many different pieces of information. The Frasier Talent Assessment Profile (F-TAP; Frasier, 1994) was designed to facilitate the process of collecting, displaying, and interpreting data from multiple sources and displaying the results.

Other methods can also be used to present multiple criteria. Some of these include using a case study approach, a profile, and a minimum score approach. More information on using each of these can be found in Chapter Five.

Test Fairness

Questions about the fairness of tests have centered on four concerns: the norms used for test interpretation, tests with large numbers of items that are high in language demands, item bias, and the purposes for which the test is used.

Norms Used for Test Interpretation

The first concern refers to the adequacy of the norms used for test interpretation. A normative score (e.g., a standard score or a percentile rank) compares an individual's performance with the performances of other individuals who took the same test. The score does not tell us anything about the individuals who make up the sample we used for comparison purposes. This sample is called the *normative sample*. To understand a person's performance on a test, an examiner must know the demographic characteristics and the abilities of the individuals who make up the normative sample (Salvia & Ysseldyke, 2001). For example, suppose a normative sample consists of a group of individuals who were identified as intellectually gifted. A person's score at the 50th percentile of this normative sample would indicate superior intelligence. On the other hand, if the normative sample consisted of individuals who were representative of the population of individuals who live in the United States, a person's score at the 50th percentile would indicate average intelligence.

To decide if a normative sample is representative, one must determine if it contains people with relevant demographic characteristics and experiences and if these are present in the same proportion as they are in the population. For example, geographic region is considered to be a relevant demographic characteristic for most tests. We know from the *Statistical Abstract of the United*

States (U.S. Bureau of the Census, 2001) that approximately 18% of school-age children live in the northeast region of the United States. Therefore, an examiner who wants to compare individuals to a test that has a normative sample representative of the United States would expect about 18% of the individuals comprising the normative sample to come from the northeast. Other relevant demographic characteristics include age, gender, and ethnicity. Finally, for a test that measures intelligence or aptitude, the individuals that comprise the normative sample should reflect the full range of intellectual ability.

Examiners will want to study the characteristics of the normative sample to determine if the relevant characteristics are present. The relevant characteristics will change depending on the type and uses of the test.

Tests With High Language Demands

The second concern is that many tests used to identify students as gifted contain large numbers of linguistically loaded items. Bernal (1981) asserted that culturally and linguistically diverse students must overcome language and cultural barriers before they may demonstrate high intellectual potential and specific academic aptitude. For these students, taking tests with large numbers of items that are language-based creates an unneeded barrier. He suggested that examiners use culture-free and nonverbal tests or measures. We discuss using nonverbal tests and measures in more detail in Chapter Two.

Ortiz and Volkoff (1987) have found that Hispanic youngsters perform better on individually administered intelligence measures such as the Wechsler Intelligence Scales for Children—Fourth Edition (Wechsler, 2003) than on group intelligence measures such as the Otis-Lennon School Abilities Test (Otis & Lennon, 1996). They concluded that group intelligence and achievement tests that require a high level of general information or reading comprehension are socially biased since economically disadvantaged and culturally/linguistically diverse students often lack the exposure to educational materials in their home.

In summary, tests that have high verbal content should not be used to identify culturally and linguistically diverse students and students from economically disadvantaged backgrounds as gifted. Tests should be nonverbal or individually administered.

Item Bias

The third concern is that tests may contain items that are biased against certain cultural and socioeconomic groups. This section will discuss the term *bias* from two perspectives. The first is in a social sense (a review of an item by experts found that it fosters stereotypes). The second is in a statistical sense (the statistical procedure showed that the item is biased).

In the social sense, we might find that an item is biased because the low performance by one group is capitalizing unfairly on knowledge and skills that are not part of that group's culture. For example, suppose African American students score lower as a group on an achievement test and that this is true regardless of ability level. This means that two students, one White and one African American, with the same ability level will score differently on the test. In this case, we would want to check the items on that test to determine if some are requiring knowledge that is alien to the African American culture. In fact, this should be completed on all tests that are norm-referenced as part of the test development.

To detect item bias, test developers should carry out three steps. First, items on the test should be reviewed by experts in the field to ensure that they do not foster stereotypes, do not contain ethnocentric or gender-based assumptions, and are not offensive to the examinee (Ramsey, 1993). Items that do not pass this review should be deleted. Second, test developers should subject their items to a differential item functioning (DIF) analysis, which requires that the items be analyzed using some statistical procedure. The purpose of a DIF analysis is to determine if equally able individuals from different groups have different probabilities of answering an item correctly. If the statistical procedure used finds that the two groups do have different probabilities of answering an item correctly, then we say the item contains DIF. Third, items that are identified as containing DIF should be reviewed to determine if the content of the item implies bias in the social sense. According to Camilli (1993) this is an important step because the presence of DIF (bias in the statistical sense)

47

does not necessarily imply bias. In order to be biased in the social sense, the differences in the performance on the item by different groups must be due to the test measuring knowledge and skills unrelated to what the test is supposed to be measuring. For example, if a test purports to measure intelligence, an item that requires an examinee to have excellent fine motor skills would be biased against individuals with poor fine motor skills. All items that are determined to be biased in the social sense should be eliminated or deleted.

Purpose of the Test Results

No matter how much we make sure that the previous three conditions have been met, if the test is used for a purpose for which it was not designed, then it is not fair. In an earlier chapter, we indicated that test validity is the responsibility of both the test developer and the examiner. Test fairness is also the responsibility of both parties. The examiner must make sure that the test he or she uses is appropriate for its intended purposes. In other words, the examiner must use assessments that match the educational program in which a student will be placed. For example, an examiner would not use the results of an English test to place a student in a gifted mathematics class. As another example, an examiner would not use an assessment that requires an advanced level of reading to assess kindergarten students for a gifted program.

A final step, then, in determining test fairness is to evaluate the outcome of the assessment process to determine the degree to which it is benefiting the individuals being assessed. In the case of gifted education, the school district will want to ensure that the program in which students are being placed as a result of assessment is of benefit to those students.

48

Summary

In summary, school districts will want to first make sure that educators and other professionals do not hold negative attitudes about economically disadvantaged and culturally/linguistically diverse students. If they do, then they should engage in advocacy efforts designed to promote the recognition of indicators of potential in these students and to provide opportunities for them to show their strengths. School districts should also use multiple measures that are both qualitative and quantitative from multiple sources. Next, school district personnel should examine all norm-referenced tests' technical manuals to ensure that the normative sample is representative and that item bias studies have been conducted. When testing economically disadvantaged and culturally/linguistically diverse students, examiners should use nonverbal or individually administered intelligence or aptitude measures. Finally, school district personnel will want to ensure that the students identified as gifted are benefiting from the gifted program in which they are placed. If they are not, then either the wrong students are being identified or the program is poorly designed.

CHAPTER FOUR

Technical Information Regarding Assessment

by Jennifer L. Jolly & Jennifer Robins Hall

In selecting nationally normed, standardized instruments for the identification of gifted and talented students, educators need to use certain guiding principles to ensure the assessment matching the student population being considered is reliable and valid for the purpose.

These questions are important to ask before selecting any assessment:

1. What is the purpose for the assessment?
2. Is the assessment valid for this purpose?
3. Is the test reliable?
4. What is the age of the instrument?
5. Does the sample used to norm the test reflect current national census data and the school district's population?
6. What type of scores does the instrument provide?
7. How is the test administered?
8. Are there qualified personnel to administer the instrument?
9. What is the cost of the instrument?

This chapter will address each of these questions and provide a review of instruments published within the past 10 years that are often used in the identification of gifted and talented students.

While many tests have been developed for aptitude and achievement, fewer have been developed for creativity and leadership. Nearly

35 of the tests reviewed were classified as either achievement or aptitude, while only 6 related to the areas of creativity, leadership, and the arts. There is an obvious need for more instruments in these latter areas that are included in the national definition for gifted and talented.

Technical Qualities

Test reviews detail technical qualities reported by the technical manual or, in some cases, a test review published by test publishers or the Buros *Mental Measurements Yearbook* (see the source that is noted for each test in Table 4.1). Each review includes the purpose of the test, validity, reliability, age of the instrument, the norming sample, types of scores, administration format, and qualifications of testing personnel. Tests chosen to be included in the reviews were (a) normed within the last 10 years; (b) cited in journals, textbooks, and other publications concerning gifted and talented students; and (c) commonly used by districts nationwide to identify gifted and talented students. Standardization and technical properties are provided to help educators make informed decisions when choosing assessments for gifted and talented identification.

Purpose

If the purpose for the assessment is identification of gifted and talented students, then the test developers should state that the instrument may be used in this way or at least have a research study that shows that the instrument discriminates between students who are gifted and nongifted. In addition, the test should relate to the school district's definition of giftedness and to their program. For example, if the program is focused on general intellectual ability, then the test should assess intelligence; if focused on leadership, then the test should assess leadership. For validity purposes, a test should be used only as its developers intended. Each test review in Table 4.1 includes the test developers' intended purpose of the test and primary focus: achievement in reading, language, mathematics, or all areas; general intellectual ability; creativity, leadership, fine arts, performing arts, visual arts, or motivation.

Validity

In addition to reporting how well the tests relate to the described purpose, the technical manual should also provide validity studies that show that the test represents the domain or gifted area (e.g., content validity), that it represents the theory or underlying models (e.g., construct validity), and that it predicts the student's performance on other assessments, products, or performances (e.g., criterion-prediction validity).

With content validity, the technical manual describes how the test questions adequately cover the domain under consideration. For example, to assess a student's knowledge of reading comprehension, a measure would include questions that address the understanding of a short story or paragraph (Anastasi & Urbina, 1997; Kubiszyn & Borich, 2000).

Similar to content validity, construct validity describes not only how well the assessment covers the domain, but also how well it translates the construct (Trochim, 2000). For example, if creativity is defined as fluency, flexibility, originality, and elaboration, the test should assess each of these factors.

Not only should the test possess face validity, an overall appearance of what the test purports to measure, but the authors should have conducted a study that shows each factor indeed exists (Anastasi & Urbina, 1997). Criterion-prediction validity indicates if the instrument can effectively predict a student's performance on a measure that assesses the same area in a similar way. For example the Test of Nonverbal Intelligence (TONI-3) and the Naglieri Nonverbal Ability Test (NNAT) are both measures of nonverbal intelligence. The correlation coefficient reported between the TONI-3 and NNAT is .63, which is an expected moderate relationship. A criterion coefficient between .40 and .60 is moderate, while .70 and above indicates a strong correlation. As the validity coefficient nears 1.00, the test becomes more accurate in predicting the criterion (Gregory, 2000). High scores on one should most likely predict high scores on the other because they are both sampling nonverbal intelligent behaviors.

Similarly, high scores on a school aptitude test such as the SAT should predict a high GPA in college.

In both of these cases, performance should be related to the construct of the test (e.g., achievement, intelligence), not to the background of the student. For this reason, the technical manual will also report whether a test is fair to certain groups of subjects. Subject characteristics such as ethnicity, gender, and socioeconomic background are considered to ensure that the test is not biased in favor of or against certain groups. If an assessment does not provide validity studies that relate to its purpose, it should not be used.

For each assessment, we identified if there were adequate studies related to content, construct, and criterion-prediction validity (see individual test reviews) and also reported if the test reported bias studies.

Reliability

Reliability refers to how consistently the assessment (a) measures the same trait or construct (e.g., internal consistency), (b) yields the same score after repeated administrations (e.g., stability reliability), and (c) is scored similarly between two or more observers or raters (e.g., interrater/scorer reliability).

With internal consistency, each item is related to one another and the overall score. In this way, the developer of the test ensures that all of the items consistently measure the same trait or characteristic (Kubiszyn & Borich, 2000). Reliability coefficients reflect the relationship between two sets of scores and range between 0 and 1, with 1 representing a perfect relationship and 0 representing no relationship. Some relationships may even be negative so that a high score on one test may relate to a negative sore on another test. For example, creativity tests and intelligence tests may or may not relate to one another because of the ways in which the constructs are defined. Generally, a desirable reliability coefficient for an identification measure typically falls in the .80s or .90s. Cronbach alpha is generally used to determine internal consistency reliability and is often reported in technical manuals (Anastasi & Urbina, 1997).

Interscorer reliability is reported when subjective measures are included in a test. A correlation coefficient of .80 and above for interscorer reliability is considered acceptable. Internal consis-

54

tency, test-retest reliability, and interscorer coefficients are listed for each of the reviewed instruments.

Age of Instrument

Since the demographics of the United States are constantly changing along with school populations, a norming sample that is older than 12 years should be used with great caution (Kubiszyn & Borich, 2000). When reviewing each of the instruments, the date of the most recent norms were reported, not when the test was last published (i.e., a test may have a new revision that updates the manual, but does not update the norms).

Norming Sample

The demographic characteristics of the students in the school district's population should be represented in the norming population, which should relate to the most recent census data. For example, if the students being assessed are in an urban school district, urban school district students should be included in the norming sample; if rural, then a rural district's students would be included. Sample characteristics are included in each test review. These characteristics included age, community type, ethnicity, family income, gender, geographic region, race, residence, socioeconomic status, and special populations. When a school district varies greatly from the national norms (e.g., the majority of the students are Hispanic), local norms might be calculated so that a more meaningful comparison can be made. The publisher of the test may provide assistance in calculating local norms (Kubiszyn & Borich, 2000). Remember that the size of the sample is not as important as how representative it is. Samples for standardization were considered representative if the technical manual reported five or more characteristics of the sample.

Types of Scores

55

Using data from the norming sample, tables are constructed and can include raw scores, percentile ranks, standard scores, age or grade equivalent scores, and stanines.

Raw scores are simply the number of items correctly answered and are therefore not comparable across tests, just as grades are not comparable across teachers. Percentile scores are a rank ordering of students who took the same test. For example, a student who scores at the 95th percentile is performing as well or better than 95% of the other students who took the same test. Percentile ranks are also not comparable to percentile ranks on other tests since they rank order students' performance on one test only (Anastasi & Urbina, 1997).

Standard scores also compare a student's performance to other students of the same age or grade level. However, the scores are not in an order like percentile ranks; rather, they are expressed in standard deviation units on a normal curve. Standard scores are therefore comparable across tests since they are based on a common distribution: the bell-shaped curve. Most intelligence tests have a mean or average score of 100 with a standard deviation of 15. Stanines are a specific type of standard scores based on the normal curve that have been divided into nine equal sections. Stanines range from 1 to 9 and are useful in describing broad bands of performance (in Chapter Five, Table 5.2 describes how to interpret these scores).

Grade- and age-equivalent scores should be avoided when comparing scores across tests. Grade-equivalent scores are estimates that are used to extrapolate a student's achievement score based on a performance at his or her grade level. They have several shortcomings. First, instruction from grade to grade, school to school, district to district, and state to state are unequal and therefore not comparable. In addition, if a student in the fourth grade scores a grade equivalent of 7.5 in math, it does not mean that this student has mastered the math concepts taught in the seventh grade or can do math at the seventh-grade level since the score is simply an estimate based on current performance. Age-equivalent scores are similar to grade-equivalent scores. Since children develop at different rates academically, socially, and physically, these scores should also not be used for comparison purposes across tests (Kubiszyn & Borich, 2000).

Since school districts will be using multiple assessments in identifying gifted students, standard scores are important for comparison purposes. Types of scores are provided along with subtests and composites for each test. A subtest is a single test, while a composite is comprised of two or more tests within the same test.

Administration

The test manual should indicate whether a test should be administered individually, in large group or small group, or in either setting. A group-administered test allows more students to take a test at a specific time and also cuts back on the time needed to complete the overall test administration. Tests reviewed are categorized as individual or group-administered.

Qualification of Personnel

Who will administer and interpret test data? Does the district have access to a qualified person who can administer and confidently interpret the test data? The answers to these questions are important when considering the selection of test instruments. For example, the Woodcock Johnson III requires a licensed school psychologist to administer the instrument, while a test such as the Iowa Test of Basic Skills can be administered by a classroom teacher.

User qualifications are indicated by an A, B, or C. The levels are defined as such:

A: The minimum level of competency for test use, A, necessitates that users have working knowledge of testing and measurement gained through an introductory graduate course on measurement in conjunction with applied experience.

B: The intermediate level of competency for test use, B, necessitates that users have a higher level of abilities and skills. One or more graduate courses on the specific type of test (e.g., achievement, aptitude) being administered are required for test users.

C: The highest level of competency for test use, C, necessitates that users have at least one graduate-level course

57

Table 4.1

Summary of Tests Reviewed

Name	Norm Date	Sample Size	Rep. Sample
Cognitive Abilities Test Form 6	2000	180,538	yes
Comprehensive Test of Nonverbal Intelligence	1995–1996	2,901	yes
Das Naglieri Cognitive Assessment System	1993–1996	3,072	yes
Gifted and Talented Evaluation Scales	1995	1,083	yes
Gifted Evaluation Scale–2nd Edition	1997–1998	1,439	yes
Iowa Tests of Basic Skills, Forms K, L, & M	1992 / 1995	263,402	yes
Iowa Tests of Educational Development Forms A and B	2000	96,146	yes
Kaufman Test of Educational Achievement/Normative Update	1995–1996	6,613	yes
Khatena-Morse Multitalent Perceptual Inventory	1994	6,000	no
Leadership Skills Inventory	1999	452	no
Leiter International Performance Scale–R	1995	2,411	yes
Naglieri Nonverbal Ability Test	2002	1,585	yes
Oral and Written Language Scales	1992–1993	1,985	yes
Otis Lennon School Ability Test–7th Edition	1995	463,000	no
Peabody Individual Achievement Test–Revised Normative Update	1995–1996	6,613	yes
Peabody Picture Vocabulary Test–III	1994	2,725	yes
Scales for Identifying Gifted Students	2002–2003	3,531	no
Scales for Rating Behavioral Characteristics of Superior Students–Revised	2001	572	no
Screening Assessment for Gifted Elementary Students–2nd Edition	2001	5,313	yes
Stanford Achievement Test–9th Edition	1995	450,000	no
Stanford Binet Intelligence Scales–5th Edition	2001–2002	4,800	yes
Test of Achievement and Proficiency Forms K, L, M	1992 / 1995	NG	yes
Test of Early Language Development–3rd Edition	1996–97	1,309	yes
Test of Early Mathematics Ability–3rd Edition	2000–2001	1,228	yes
Test of Early Reading Ability–3rd Edition	1999–2000	875	yes
Test of Early Written Language–2nd Edition	1996	1,479	yes
Test of Language Development Intermediate–3rd Edition	1996	779	yes
Test of Language Development Primary–3rd Edition	1996	1,000	yes
Test of Mathematical Abilities for Gifted Students	1997	2,702	yes
Test of Nonverbal Intelligence–3rd Edition	1995–96	3,451	yes
Test of Reading Comprehension–3rd Edition	1995	1,962	yes
Test of Written Language–3rd Edition	1995	2,217	yes
Universal Nonverbal Intelligence Test	1998	2,100	yes
Wechsler Individual Achievement Test–2nd Edition	1999–2001	6,550	yes
Wechsler Intelligence Scale for Children–4th Edition	2000	2,200	yes
Woodcock Johnson III	1996–1999	8,818	yes
Woodcock Reading Mastery Tests–Revised Normative Update	1995–1996	3,700	yes

Note. NG = not given in review; NR = not reported in test's technical manual

Control for Bias	Internal Consistency	Test–Retest	Interscorer	Validity	Source
yes	.85–.98	.69–.87	NR	yes	Technical Manual
yes	.79–.97	.79–.94	.95–.99	yes	Technical Manual
no	.64–.96	.63–.93	NR	yes	Technical Manual
yes	.95–.97	.42–.92	.42–.98	yes	Technical Manual
no	.92–.97	.86–.93	.69–.91	yes	Technical Manual
yes	.59–.90s	NG	NG	yes	Test Review–Buros
yes	.83–.98	.63–.89	NR	yes	Technical Manual
no	.80s–.90s	.80s–.90s	NG	yes	Test Review–AGS
no	.41–.92	.60–.95	.95–1.0	yes	Technical Manual
no	NR	NR	NR	NR	Technical Manual
yes	.75–.93	.88–.93	NR	yes	Technical Manual
no	.88–.95	.68–.78	NR	yes	Technical Manual
no	.77–.95	.87–.90	0.95	yes	Technical Manual
no	.63–.97	NG	NG	yes	Test Review–Buros
yes	.60–.90s	.80s–.90s	.58–.67	yes	Test Review–AGS
yes	.86–.98	.91–.94	NG	yes	Test Review–AGS
yes	.85–.98	.58–.93	.43–.60	yes	Technical Manual
no	.84–.97	NR	.50–.65	yes	Technical Manual
yes	.77–.96	.78–.97	.91–.99	yes	Technical Manual
yes	.70s–.90s	.70s–.80s	.70s–.90s	yes	Test Review–Buros
yes	.72–.98	.66–.95	.74–.98	yes	Technical Manual
yes	.85–.95	NG	NG	yes	Test Review–Buros
yes	.80–.97	.80–.98	.99	yes	Technical Manual
yes	.92–.99	.82–.93	NR	yes	Technical Manual
yes	.79–.97	.86–.99	.99	yes	Technical Manual
no	.90–.99	.82–.94	.92–.99	yes	Test Review–Buros
yes	.80–.96	.83–.96	.94–.97	yes	Technical Manual
no	.75–.96	.77–.92	.99	yes	Technical Manual
yes	.81–.92	.84–.94	.99	yes	Technical Manual
yes	.89–.97	.89–.94	.99	yes	Technical Manual
yes	.83–.98	.79–.88	.87–.98	yes	Technical Manual
yes	.69–.97	.72–.94	.80–.97	yes	Technical Manual
no	.84–.95	.74–.91	NG	yes	Test Review–Buros
no	.71–.99	.81–.99	.94–.98	yes	Technical Manual
no	.65–.97	.76–.93	.95–.98	yes	Technical Manual
yes	.41–.99	.35–.98	.71–.99	yes	Technical Manual
no	.54–.99	NR	NR	yes	Technical Manual

specific to the test being administered. For example, a person administering the Woodcock Johnson III, an achievement test, is required to have completed a course in administering this specific measure.

Regardless of the rating, all professionals should have a basic knowledge of psychological tests and measurements so that they understand the importance of standardized procedures and confidentiality when administering and interpreting assessment instruments.

Table 4.1 contains a list and summary of tests reviewed in the following pages of the chapter.

CAS

Name:	Das Naglieri Cognitive Assessment System
Author(s):	Naglieri, J. A., & Das, J. P.
Publisher:	Riverside Publishing, 8420 Bryn Mawr Ave., Chicago, IL 60631-3476

Scoring Information

Subtests:	Matching Numbers, Planned Codes, Planned Connections, Expressive Attention, Receptive Attention, Nonverbal Matrices, Verbal-Spatial Relations, Figure Memory, Word Series, Sentence Repetition, Speech Rate, Sentence Questions
Composite(s):	Full Scale Standard Score

Technical Information

Standardization

Size:	3,072 in 68 sites across the United States; 2,200 comprised the normative sample and an additional 872 who participated in reliability validity studies
Sample char.:	age, classroom placement, community setting, educational classification, gender, Hispanic origin, parental education attainment, race, region

Reliability

Internal consistency:	Subtests:	.64–.96
	Composite(s):	.95–.96
Test-Retest:	Subtests:	.63–.84
	Composite(s):	.89–.93

Validity

Content:	Yes
Construct:	correlation with achievement, factor analysis, correlation with aptitude, group differentiation
Criterion:	.06–.76

CoGAT Form 6

Mame:	Cognitive Abilities Test Form 6
Author(s):	Lohman, D. F., & Hagen, E. P.
Publisher:	Riverside Publishing, 8420 Bryn Mawr Ave., Chicago, IL 60631-3476

Scoring Information

Subtests: *Primary Ed.:* Oral Vocabulary, Verbal Reasoning, Relational Concepts, Quantitative Concepts, Figure Classification and Matrices; *Multilevel Ed.:* Verbal Classification, Sentence Completion, Verbal Analogies, Quantitative Relations, Number Series, Equation Building, Figure Classification, Figure Analogies, Figure Analysis

Composite(s): Verbal, Quantitative, Nonverbal, and Composite

Technical Information

Standardization

Size: 180,538 (total); 149,798 (grades K–8), 30,740 (grades 9–12) in 50 states and Washington, DC

Sample char.: diocese size, ethnicity, geographic region, K–12 enrollment, race, SES, students in special groups

Reliability

Internal consistency: Subtests: not reported
Composite(s): .85–.98

Test-Retest: Subtests: not reported
Composite(s): .69–.87

Validity

Content: Yes

Construct: correlations with achievement, correlations with ability, subtest correlation, item analysis, factor analysis, bias studies

Criterion: .54–.87

C-TONI

Name:	Comprehensive Test of Nonverbal Intelligence
Author(s):	Hammill, D. D., Pearson, N. A., & Wiederholt, J. L.
Publisher:	PRO-ED, 8700 Shoal Creek Blvd., Austin, TX 78756-6897

Scoring Information

Subtests:	Pictorial Analogies, Geometric Analogies, Pictorial Categories, Geometric Categories, Pictorial Sequence, Geometric Sequences
Composite(s):	Pictorial Nonverbal Intell. Composite, Geometric Nonverbal Intell., Nonverbal Intell.

Technical Information

Standardization

Size:	2,901 persons (2,129 students and 772 adults) in 30 states and the District of Columbia
Sample char.:	disabling conditions, educational attainment of parents, ethnicity, family income, gender, geographic region, race, residence,

Reliability

Internal consistency:	Subtests:	.79–.95
	Composite(s):	.91–.97
Test–Retest:	Subtests:	.79–.89
	Composite(s):	.87–.94
Interscorer:	Subtests:	.95–.99
	Composite(s):	.98–.99

Validity

Content:	yes
Construct:	age differentiation, group differentiation, subtest correlations, factor analysis, item validity, bias studies
Criterion:	.32–.90

63

GATES

Name:	Gifted and Talented Evaluation Scales
Author(s):	Gilliam, J. E., Carpenter, B. O., & Christensen, J. R.
Publisher:	PRO-ED, 8700 Shoal Creek Blvd., Austin, TX 78757-6897

Scoring Information

Subtests:	Intellectual Ability, Academic Skills, Creativity, Leadership, Artistic Talent
Composite(s):	n/a

Technical Information

Standardization

Size:	1,083 subjects in 32 states and Canada
Sample char.:	age, ethnicity, gender, geographic region, race, residence, school, SES

Reliability

	Normal subjects	Gifted subjects
Internal cons:	Subtests: .96–97 Composite(s): n/a	Subtests: .95–.97 Composite(s): n/a
Test-Retest:	Subtests: .69–.92 Composite(s): n/a	Subtests: .42–.87 Composite(s): n/a
Interscorer	Subtests: .69–.92 Composite(s): n/a	Subtests: .42–.87 Composite(s): n/a

Validity

Content:	Yes
Construct:	subtest correlations, item validity, group discrimination
Criterion:	NS–.92

GES-2

Name:	Gifted Evaluation Scale–Second Edition
Author(s):	McCarney, S. B., & Anderson, P. D.
Publisher:	Hawthorne Educational Services, 800 Gray Oak Dr., Columbia, OH 65201

Scoring Information

Subtests:	Intellectual ability, Creativity, Specific Academic Aptitude, Leadership Ability, Performing and Visual Arts, and Motivation Profile
Composite(s):	Quotient

Technical Information

Standardization
Size:	1,439 students from 15 states
Sample char.:	ethnicity, gender, geographic area, parent education, residence

Reliability
Internal consistency:	Subtests:	.92–.97
	Composite(s):	.95
Test-Retest:	Subtests:	.86–.93
	Composite(s):	.93
Interscorer	Subtests:	.69–.79
	Composite(s):	.91

Validity
Content:	Yes
Construct:	subtest correlation, item validity, group differentiation
Criterion:	.74–.86

ITBS Forms K, L, & M

Name:	Iowa Tests of Basic Skills Forms K, L, & M
Author(s):	Hoover, H., Hieronymous, A., Frisbie, D., & Dunbar, S.
Publisher:	Riverside Publishing, 8420 Bryn Mawr Ave., Chicago, IL 60631-3476

Scoring Information

Derived scores available:	percentile ranks, standard scores, grade equivalents
Subtests:	Listening, Word Analysis, Vocabulary, Reading, Language, Mathematics, Science, Social Studies, Sources of Information
Composite(s):	Composite

Technical Information

Standardization

Size:	136,934 (1992); 126,468 (1995)
Sample char.:	nationally representative sample of schools (see manual)

Reliability

Internal consistency:	Subtests:	.59–.90s
	Composite(s):	above .90
Test-Retest:	Subtests:	Not given
	Composite(s):	Not given

Validity

Content:	Yes
Construct:	correlations with subtests, correlations with cognitive ability
Criterion:	Concurrent validity: .80s

ITED Forms A and B

Name:	Iowa Tests of Educational Development Forms A and B
Author(s):	Forsyth, R., Ansley, T., Feldt, L., & Alnot, S.
Publisher:	Riverside Publishing, 8420 Bryn Mawr Ave., Chicago, IL 60631-3476

Scoring Information

Subtests:	Vocabulary, Reading Comprehension, Language: Revising Written Materials, Spelling, Mathematics: Concepts and Problem Solving, Computation, Analysis of Social Studies Materials, Analysis of Science Materials, Sources of Information.
Composite(s):	Complete Battery, Core Battery

Technical Information

Standardization

Size	96,146 students in 50 states and the District of Columbia
Sample char.:	diocese size, disability status, district enrollment, ethnicity, geographic region, race, SES, type of school

Reliability

Internal consistency:	Subtests:	.83–.92
	Composite(s):	.94–.98
Test-Retest:	Subtests:	.63–.84
	Composite(s):	.72–.89

Validity

Content:	Yes
Construct:	correlations with achievement
Criterion:	predictive validity: .24–.89

KTEA/NU

Name:	Kaufman Test of Educational Achievement/ Normative Update
Author(s):	Kaufman, A. & Kaufman, N.
Publisher:	American Guidance Service, 4201 Woodland Rd., Circle Pines, MN 55014-1796

Scoring Information

Subtests:	Reading, Mathematics, Spelling
Composite(s):	Brief and Comprehensive Forms

Technical Information

Standardization

Size:	6,613 children and adults (3,429 Total Age-Norm sample; 3,184 Total Grade-Norm sample)
Sample char.:	age, ethnicity, gender, geographic region, parental education, special populations

Reliability

	Comprehensive Form		Brief Form	
Internal cons.:	Subtests:	low .90s	Subtests:	mid to upper .80s
	Composite(s):	mid to upper .90s	Composite(s):	mid .90s
Test-Retest:	Subtests:	.90s	Subtests:	mid to upper .80s
	Composite(s):	.90s	Composite(s):	low .90s

Validity

Content:	Yes
Construct:	subtest correlations, correlations with achievement
Criterion:	.62–.8

Khatena-Morse

Name:	Khatena-Morse Multitalent Perceptual Inventory
Author(s):	Khatena, J., & Morse, D. T.
Publisher:	Scholastic Testing Service, 480 Meyer Rd., Bensenville, IL 60106-1617

Scoring Information

Subtests:	Artistry, Musical, Creative Imagination, Initiative Leadership
Composite(s):	Versatility Index

Technical Information

Standardization

Size:	6,000 subjects from the Northeast, South, Midwest, and West
Sample char.:	grade, region, gifted

Reliability

Internal consistency:	Subtests:	.41–.87 (for children)
		.41–.92 (for adults)
	Composite(s):	not reported
Test-Retest:	Subtests:	.60–.95
	Composite(s):	not reported
Interscorer:	Subtests:	.95–1.0

Validity

Content:	Yes
Construct:	factor analysis, correlational studies, cross-validation studies
Criterion:	.16–.42

69

LSI

Name: Leadership Skills Inventory
Author(s): Karnes, F. A., & Chauvin, J. C.
Publisher: Gifted Psychology Press, P.O. Box 5057, Scottsdale, AZ 85261

Scoring Information

Subtests: Fundamentals, Written Communication, Speech Communication, Character-Building, Decision-Making, Group Dynamics, Problem Solving, Personal Skills, and Planning
Composite(s): n/a

Technical Information

Standardization
Size: 452 in 7 states
Sample char.: not reported

Reliability

Internal consistency: Subtests: .80–.93
Composite(s): n/a

Test-Retest: Subtests: .30–.67 (for Louisiana sample only $N = 45$)
Composite(s): not reported

Validity
(cited studies that examine content, concurrent, and construct validity, but no scores were reported)
Content: not reported
Construct: not reported
Criterion: not reported

Leiter-R

Name:	Leiter International Performance Scale–Revised
Author(s):	Roid, G. H., & Miller, L. J.
Publisher:	Stoetling Co., 620 Wheat Lane, Wood Dale, IL 60191

Scoring Information

Subtests: Classification, Repeated Patterns, Sequential Order, Design Analogies, Matching, Figure-Ground, Form Completion, Picture Context, Paper Folding, Figure Rotation, Memory Span (Forward), Associative Memory, Spatial Memory, Immediate Recognition, Memory Span (Reverse), Associative Delayed Memory, Visual Coding (Symbol and Digit), Delayed Recognition, Attention-Sustained, Attention-Divided

Composite(s): Visualization, Reasoning, Attention, and Memory; IQ score

Technical Information

Standardization

Size: 2,411 total (1,719 typical children and adolescents and 692 atypical children representing 9 clinical groups from geographic regions of the United States)

Sample char.: community size, ethnicity, gender, geographic region, race, SES

Reliability

Internal consistency: Subtests: .75–.90
Composite(s): .88–.93

Test–Retest: Subtests: .88–.91
Composite(s): .88–.93

Validity

Content: Yes
Construct: correlates with ability, factor analysis, group differentiation, item analysis, bias studies
Criterion: .78–.85

71

NNAT

Name:	Naglieri Nonverbal Ability Test
Author(s):	Naglieri, J. A.
Publisher:	The Psychological Corporation, 19500 Bulverde Road, San Antonio, TX 78259

Scoring Information

Subtests: n/a
Composite(s):   Intelligence Quotient

Technical Information

Standardization
Size: 1,585 subjects from the West, Midwest, South, and Northeast
Sample char.:   age, gender, geographic region, parent education level, and race/ethnicity

Reliability
Internal consistency: Subtests: n/a
                      Composite(s):   .88–.95

Test-Retest: Subtests: n/a
                      Composite(s):   .68–.78

Validity
Content: Yes
Construct: group differentiation, correlations with ability
Criterion: .36–.78

OWLS

Name:	Oral and Written Language Scales
Author(s):	Carrow-Woolfolk, E.
Publisher:	American Guidance Services, 4201 Woodland Road, Circle Pines, MN 55014

Scoring Information

Subtests:	Conventions, Linguistics, and Content
Composite(s):	Language Composite Scores

Technical Information

Standardization
Size:	1,985 subjects representing the Northeast, South, Midwest, and West in the United States
Sample char.:	age, ethnicity, gender, geographic region, mother's educational level, race

Reliability
Internal consistency:	Subtests:	.77–.94
	Composite(s):	.90–.95
Test–Retest:	Subtests:	.87–.88
	Composite(s):	.87–.90
Interscorer	Subtests:	.95

Validity
Content:	Yes
Construct:	subtest correlations, correlations with achievement, correlations with ability, group differentiation
Criterion:	.63–.88

OLSAT (7th Edition)

Name:	Otis Lennon School Ability Test (7th Edition)
Author(s):	Otis, A. & Lennon, R.
Publisher:	Harcourt Brace Educational Measurement, 555 Academic Ct., San Antonio, TX 78204-2498

Scoring Information

Subtests:	Verbal and Nonverbal
Composite(s):	Total

Technical Information

Standardization

Size:	463,000
Sample char.:	SES, district enrollment, geographic region

Reliability

Internal consistency:	Subtests:	.63–.96
	Composite(s):	.78–.97
Test-Retest:	Subtests:	not given
	Composite(s):	not given

Validity

Content:	yes
Construct:	correlations between adjacent levels of OLSAT, correlations with achievement
Criterion:	.65–.88

PIAT-R /NU

Name:	Peabody Individual Achievement Test–Revised, Normative Update
Author(s):	Markwardt, F. C., Jr.
Publisher:	American Guidance Services, 4201 Woodland Rd., Circle Pines, MN 55014

Scoring Information

Subtests:	General Information, Reading Recognition, Reading Comprehension, Mathematics, Spelling, Written Expression
Composite(s):	Total Reading, Total Test, and Written Language Composite(s)

Technical Information

Standardization

Size:	6,613 total (3,429 Total Age-Norm sample and 3,184 Total Grade-Norm sample in 33 communities nationwide)
Sample char.:	age, ethnicity, gender, geographic region, parent educational attainment, race, SES, special populations

Reliability

Internal consistency:	Subtests:	.60s–mid-.90s
	Composite(s):	upper .90s
Test-Retest:	Subtests:	not given
	Composite(s):	Grade Norms high .80s to mid-.90s; Age Norms low to mid .90s
Intescorer:	Subtests:	.58–.67
	Composite(s):	not given

Validity

Content:	Yes
Construct:	subtest correlations, factor analysis, correlations with achievement, group differentiation, bias studies
Criterion:	.50–.72

PPVT-III

Name:	Peabody Picture Vocabulary Test–Third Edition
Author(s):	Dunn, L. M., Dunn, L, M., Williams, K. T., & Wang, J. J.
Publisher:	American Guidance Services, 4201 Woodland Rd., Circle Pines, MN 55014

Scoring Information

Subtests:	n/a
Composite(s):	Receptive Vocabulary Score

Technical Information

Standardization
Size:	2,725 subjects tested at 268 sites nationwide
Sample char.:	age, gender, geographic region, race, SES/parent education, and special populations

Reliability

Internal consistency:	Subtests:	n/a
	Composite(s):	.86–.98
Test-Retest:	Subtests:	n/a
	Composite(s):	.91–.94

Validity
Content:	Yes
Construct:	correlations with oral language, correlations with cognitive ability, bias studies
Criterion:	.62–.92

SIGS

Name:	Scales for Identifying Gifted Students/SIGS
Author(s):	Ryser, G. R., & McConnell, K.
Publisher:	Prufrock Press, P.O. Box 8813, Waco, TX 76714-8813

Scoring Information

Scales: General Intellectual Ability, Language Arts, Mathematics, Science, Social Studies, Creativity, Leadership

Technical Information

Standardization
Size: 1,055 Gifted School Rating Scale, 811 Gifted Home Rating Scale, 921 General Norms School Rating Scale, 744 General Norms Home Rating Scale collected from 23 states. Sample controlled for ethnicity, gender, geographic area, race

Reliability
Internal consistency:	.85–.98
Test-Retest:	.58–.93
Interscorer:	.43–.60

Validity
Content:	Yes
Construct:	correlations with academic achievement , correlations with intelligence, correlations with creativity, group discrimination, bias studies
Criterion:	.38–.73

Scales for Rating the Behavioral Characteristics of Superior Students

Name: Scales for Rating the Behavioral Characteristics of Superior Students

Author(s):   Renzulli, J. S., Smith, L. H., White, A. J., Callahan, C. M., Hartman, R. K., & Westberg, K. L.

Publisher: Creative Learning Press, P.O. Box 320, Mansfield Center, CT 06250

Scoring Information

Subtests: Learning, Creativity, Motivation, Leadership, Artistic, Musical, Dramatics, Communication, and Planning

Composite(s): Scale Total

Technical Information

Standardization

Size: 572 (146 males; 426 females) in 12 states

Sample char.: gender

Reliability

Internal consistency:	Subtests:	.84–.91
	Composite(s):	.97
Test-Retest:	Subtests:	not reported
	Composite(s):	not reported
Interscorer:	Subtests:	.50–.65

78

Validity

Content: Yes

Construct: exploratory analysis, factor analysis

Criterion: .40–.95

SAGES-2

Name:	Screening Assessment for Gifted Elementary Students–2nd Edition
Author(s):	Johnsen, S. K., & Corn, A. L.
Publisher:	PRO-ED, 8700 Shoal Creek Blvd., Austin, TX 78757-6897

Scoring Information

Subtests:	Mathematics/Science; Language Arts/Social Science; Reasoning (Forms K–3; 4–8)
Composite(s):	n/a

Technical Information

Standardization

Size:	5,313 persons in 28 states: 3,023 (normal sample, 1,547 in grades K–3; 1,476 in grades 4–8); 2,290 (gifted sample, 836 in grades K–3; 1,454 in grades 4–8)
Sample char.:	age, disability status, ethnicity, family income, geographic area, gender, race, residence, and parent educational attainment

Reliability

	K–3		4–8	
	Normal	Gifted	Normal	Gifted
Internal cons. Subtests:	.77–.93	.88–.94	.88–.96	.82–.93
Composite(s):	n/a	n/a	n/a	n/a

	K–3	4–8
Test-Retest:		
Subtests:	.95–.97	.78–.92
Composite(s):	n/a	n/a
Interscorer:		
Subtests:	.92–.99	.91–.97
Composite(s):	n/a	n/a

Validity

Content: Yes

Construct: age differentiation, group differentiation, subtest correlations, item validity, bias studies

Criterion: NS–.89

Stanford Achievement Test (9th Edition)

Name: Stanford Achievement Test (9th Edition)
Author(s):   Harcourt-Brace Educational Measurement
Publisher: Harcourt-Brace Educational Measurement, 555
             Academic Ct., San Antonio, TX 75204

Scoring Information

Subtests: Reading, Language, Spelling, Study Skills,
             Listening, Mathematics, Science, Social Science,
             Writing
Composite(s): Yes

Technical Information

Standardization
Size: 450,000 students
Sample char.: ethnicity, SES, urbanicity

Reliability

Internal consistency: Subtests: .70s–.90s
                      Composite(s): .70s–.90s

Test-Retest: Subtests: most in .70s–.80s
                      Composite(s): not given

Interscorer: . 70s–.90s

Validity
Content: Yes
Construct: correlations with ability
Criterion: not given

Stanford-Binet 5th Edition

Name: Stanford Binet Intelligence Scales–5th Edition
Author(s):   Roid, G. H.
Publisher: Riverside Publishing, 8420 Bryn Mawr Ave., Chicago, IL 60631-3476

Scoring Information

Derived scores avail.: standard scores, age equivalents
Subtests: Nonverbal Fluid Reasoning, Nonverbal Knowledge, Nonverbal Quantitative Reasoning, Nonverbal Visual-Spatial Processing, Nonverbal Working Memory, Verbal Fluid Reasoning, Verbal Knowledge, Verbal Quantitative Reasoning, Verbal Visual-Spatial Processing, Verbal Working Memory
Composite(s):   Full Scale IQ, Nonverbal IQ, Verbal IQ, and Abbreviated Battery IQ

Technical Information

Standardization

Size: 4,800 in the four U.S. census regions
Sample char.: age, geographic region, race/ethnicity, sex, SES

Reliability

Internal consistency:	Subtests:	.72–.98
	Composite(s):	.87–.95
Test-Retest	Subtests:	.66–.93
	Composite(s):	.84–.95
Interscorer:	Subtests:	.74–.98

Validity

Content: Yes

Construct: correlations with subtests, factor analysis, bias studies, correlations with cognitive ability

Criterion: Concurrent validity: .33–.84

TAP Forms K, L, M

Name: Tests of Achievement and Proficiency Forms K, L, M
Author(s): Scannell, D. P., Haugh, O. M., Loyd, B. H., & Risinger, F.
Publisher: Riverside Publishing, 8420 Bryn Mawr Ave., Chicago, IL 60631-3476

Scoring Information

Subtests: Vocabulary, Reading Comprehension, Written Expression, Math Concepts and Problem Solving, Math Computation, Social Studies, Science, Information Processing
Composite(s): Composite

Technical Information

Standardization
Size: Not given
Sample char.: nationally representative sample of schools (see manual)

Reliability
Internal consistency: Subtests: .85–.95 (a few above or below)
Composite(s): Not given

Test-Retest: Subtests: Not given
Composite(s): Not given

Validity
Content: Yes
Construct: correlations with cognitive ability, correlations with achievement
Criterion: not given

TELD-3

Name: Test of Early Language Development–Third Edition

Author(s):   Hresko, W. P., Reid, D. K., & Hammill, D. D.

Publisher: PRO-ED, 8700 Shoal Creek Blvd., Austin, TX 78757-6897

Scoring Information

Subtests: Receptive Language, Expressive Language

Composite(s):   Spoken Language

Technical Information

Standardization

Size: 1,309

Sample char.:   educational attainment of parents, ethnicity, family income, gender, geographic area, race, and residence

Reliability

Internal consistency: Subtests: .80–.97

                        Composite(s):   .89–.97

Test-Retest: Subtests: .80–.96

                        Composite(s):   .90–.98

Interscorer: .99

Validity

Content: Yes

Construct: age differentiation, subtest correlations, group differentiation including students with ADHD, learning disabilities delayed language and mental retardation, correlations with academic and school-related ability, correlations with intelligence, bias studies

Criterion: .30–.92

TEMA-3

Name: Test of Early Mathematics Ability–Third Edition
Author(s): Ginsburg, H. P. & Baroody, A. J.
Publisher: PRO-ED, 8700 Shoal Creek Blvd., Austin, TX 78757-6897

Scoring Information

Subtests: n/a
Composite(s): Total Score-Math Ability

Technical Information

Standardization
Size: 1,228
Sample char.: educational attainment of parents, ethnicity, family income, gender, geographic area, and race

Reliability
Internal consistency: Subtests: n/a
Composite(s): .92–.99

Test-Retest: Subtests: n/a
Composite(s): .82–.93

Validity
Content: Yes
Construct: age differentiation, group differentiation including students with low mathematics achievement, item validity, bias studies
Criterion: .54–.91

TERA-3

Name:	Test of Early Reading Ability–Third Edition
Author(s):	Reid, D. K., Hresko, W. P., & Hammill, D. D.
Publisher:	PRO-ED, 8700 Shoal Creek Blvd., Austin, TX 78757-6897

Scoring Information

Subtests:	Alphabet, Conventions, Meaning
Composite(s):	TERA-3 Reading Quotient

Technical Information

Standardization
Size:	875
Sample char.:	educational attainment of parents, ethnicity, family income, gender, geographic area, race, and residence

Reliability
Internal consistency:	Subtests:	.79–95
	Composite(s):	.91–.97
Test-Retest:	Subtests:	.86–98
	Composite(s):	.91–.99
Interscorer:	.99	

Validity
Content:	Yes
Construct:	age differentiation, subtest correlations, group differentiation including students with learning disabilities, reading disabilities, and language impairments, correlations with academic achievement, correlations with intelligence, confirmatory factor analysis, bias studies
Criterion:	.36–.98

87

TEWL-2

Name:	Test of Early Written Language–2nd Edition
Author(s):	Hresko, W. P., Herron, S. R., & Peak, P. K.
Publisher:	PRO-ED, 8700 Shoal Creek Blvd., Austin, TX 78757-6897

Scoring Information

Subtests:	Basic Writing, Contextual Writing, and Global Writing
Composite(s):	n/a

Technical Information

Standardization
Size:	1,479
Sample char.:	age, gender, race, ethnicity, residence, and geographic region

Reliability
Internal consistency:	Subtests:	.90–.99
	Composite(s):	n/a
Test–Retest:	Subtests:	.82–.94
	Composite(s	n/a
Interscorer:	Subtests:	.92–.99
	Composite(s):	n/a

Validity
Content:	Yes
Construct:	correlations with cognitive ability
Criterion:	Predicative Validity: .62–.69

TOLD-I:3

Name:	Test of Language Development Intermediate (3rd edition)
Author(s):	Hammill D. D., & Newcomer, P. L.
Publisher:	PRO-ED, 8700 Shoal Creek Blvd., Austin, TX 78757-6897

Scoring Information

Subtests:	Sentence Combining, Picture Vocabulary, Word Ordering, Generals, Grammatic Comprehension, Malapropisms
Composite(s):	Spoken Language, Semantics, Syntax, Listening, and Speaking

Technical Information

Standardization
Size: 779 persons in 23 states
Sample char.: age, disability status, educational attainment of parents, ethnicity, family income, gender, geographic area, race, and residence

Reliability
Internal consistency: Subtests: .80–.97
                       Composite(s):   .92–.96

Test-Retest: Subtests: .83–.93
                       Composite(s):   .94–.96

Interscorer: .94–.97

Validity
Content: Yes
Construct: subtest correlations, age differentiation, group differentiation, correlations with achievement, factor analysis, item validity, correlations with ability, bias studies
Criterion: .58–.86 (subtests) and .74–.88 (Composite[s])

TOLD-P:3

Name:	Test of Language Development–Primary (3rd Edition)
Author(s):	Newcomer, P. L., & Hammill D. D.
Publisher:	PRO-ED, 8700 Shoal Creek Blvd., Austin, TX 78757-6897

Scoring Information

Subtests:	Picture Vocabulary, Relation Vocabulary, Oral Vocabulary, Grammatic Understanding, Sentence Imitation, Grammatic Completion, Word Discrimination, Phonemic Analysis, Word Articulation
Composite(s):	Listening, Organizing, Speaking, Semantics, Syntax, Spoken Language

Technical Information

Standardization

Size:	1,000 persons in 28 states
Sample char.:	disability status, educational attainment of parents, ethnicity, family income, gender, geographic area, race, and rural vs. urban status

Reliability

Internal consistency:	Subtests:	.75–.94
	Composite(s):	.89–.96
Test-Retest:	Subtests:	.77–.90
	Composite(s):	.82–.92
Interscorer	Subtests	.99
	Composite(s):	.99

90

Validity

Content:	Yes
Construct:	age differentiation, group differentiation, subtest correlations, factor analysis, item validity
Criterion:	NS–.97

TOMAGS

Name:	Test of Mathematical Abilities for Gifted Students
Author(s):	Ryser, G. R., & Johnsen, S. K.
Publisher:	PRO-ED, 8700 Shoal Creek Blvd., Austin, TX 78757-6897

Scoring Information

Subtests:	n/a
Composite(s):	Primary Level and Intermediate Level

Technical Information

Standardization

Size:	1,572 normal sample (935 Prim. Level; 637 Int. Level) in 11 states; 1,130 gifted sample (617 Prim. Level; 513 Int. Level)
Sample char.:	age, educational attainment, ethnicity, family income, gender, geographic area, race, and residence

Reliability

	Primary Level		Intermediate Level	
	Normal	Gifted	Normal	Gifted
Internal cons.:				
Subtests:	n/a	n/a	n/a	n/a
Composite(s):	.81–.92	.81–.90	.81–.90	.82–.85

	Primary Level	Intermediate Level
Test-Retest:		
Subtests:	n/a	n/a
Composite(s):	.84	.94
Interscorer:		
Subtests:	n/a	n/a
Composite(s):	.99	.99

Validity

Content:	Yes
Construct:	factor analysis, group differentiation, item validity, bias studies
Criterion:	Primary Level .62–.73; Intermediate Level .44–.67

TONI-3

Name:	Test of Nonverbal Intelligence 3rd Edition
Author(s):	Brown, L., Sherbenou, R., & Johnsen, S.
Publisher:	PRO-ED, 8700 Shoal Creek Blvd., Austin, TX 78757-6897

Scoring Information

Subtests	n/a
Composite(s):	Quotient

Technical Information

Standardization
Size:	3,451 persons in 20 states
Sample char.:	age, disability status, educational attainment of parents, educational attainment of school-age siblings, educational attainment of adult subjects, ethnicity, family income of adult subjects, family income of school-age subjects, gender, geographic region, race, residence

Reliability
Internal consistency:	Subtests:	n/a
	Composite(s):	.89–.97
Test-Retest:	Subtests:	n/a
	Composite(s):	.89–.94
Interscorer:	Subtest:	n/a
	Composite:	.99

Validity
Content:	Yes
Construct	age differentiation, correlation with school achievement, multiple correlations with intelligence, factor analysis, item discrimination, group differentiation, bias studies
Criterion:	.51–.76

TORC-3

Name:	Test of Reading Comprehension–Third Edition
Author(s):	Brown, V. L., Hammill, D. D., & Wiederholt, J. L.
Publisher:	PRO-ED, 8700 Shoal Creek Blvd., Austin, TX 78757-6897

Scoring Information

Subtests:	General Vocab.; Syntactic Similarities; Paragraph Reading; Sentence Sequencing; Content Area Vocabularies: Mathematics, Social Studies, and Science; Reading the Directions of Schoolwork
Composite(s):	Reading Comprehension

Technical Information

Standardization
Size: 1,962
Sample char.: ethnicity, gender, geographic area, residence, race

Reliability

Internal consistency:	Subtests:	.83–.95
	Composite(s):	.96–.98
Test-Retest:	Subtests:	.79–.88
	Composite(s):	.85
Interscorer:	.87–.98	

Validity
Content: Yes
Construct: age differentiation; subtest correlations; group differentiation, including students who are low achieving, are receiving residential treatment, are poor readers, have language disabilities, have learning disabilities, or are dyslexic; correlations with academic achievement; correlations with aptitude; correlations with intelligence; bias studies
Criterion: .22–87

94

TOWL-3

Name:	Test of Written Language–Third Edition
Author(s):	Hammill, D. D., & Larsen, S. C.
Publisher:	PRO-ED, 8700 Shoal Creek Blvd., Austin, TX 78757-6897

Scoring Information

Subtests:	Vocabulary, Spelling, Style, Logical Sentences, Sentence Combining, Contextual Conventions, Contextual Language, Story Construction
Composite(s):	Contrived Writing, Spontaneous Writing, Overall Writing

Technical Information

Standardization
Size:	2,217 persons in 25 states
Sample char.:	educational attainment of parents, ethnicity, family income, gender, geographic area, race, and residence

Reliability
Internal consistency:	Subtests:	.69–.91
	Composite(s):	.91–.97
Test-Retest:	Subtests:	.72–.93
	Composite(s):	.83–.94
Interscorer:	.80–.97	

Validity
Content:	Yes
Construct:	age differentiation, subtest correlations, group differentiation including students with learning disabilities and speech impairments, correlations with academic achievement, correlations with intelligence, exploratory factor analysis, bias studies
Criterion:	.34–.69

UNIT

Name: Universal Nonverbal Intelligence Test
Author(s): Bracken, B. A., & McCallum, S. R.
Publisher: Riverside Publishing, 8420 Bryn Mawr Ave., Chicago, IL 60631-3476

Scoring Information

Subtests: Symbolic Memory, Cube Design, Spatial Memory, Analogic Reasoning, Object Memory, Mazes
Composite(s): Full Scale IQ

Technical Information

Standardization
Size: 2,100
Sample char.: gender, race, Hispanic origin, region, parent education, community, classroom placement, special education, and gifted

Reliability
Internal consistency: Subtests: not given
                     Composite(s): .84–.95

Test-Retest: Subtests: not given
                     Composite(s): .74–.91

Validity
Content: Yes
Construct: correlation with nonverbal measures
Criterion .54–.66

WIAT II

Name: Wechsler Individual Achievement Test (2nd Edition)
Author(s): The Psychological Corporation
Publisher: The Psychological Corporation, 19500 Bulverde Rd., San Antonio, TX 78259

Scoring Information

Subtests: Word Reading, Reading Comprehension, Pseudoword Decoding, Numerical Operations, Mathematics Reasoning, Spelling, Written Expression, Listening Comprehension, Oral Expression
Composite(s): Reading, Mathematics, Written Language, Oral Language

Technical Information

Standardization
Size: 6,550 total (3,600 [grade] and 2,950 [age])
Sample char.: age, ethnicity, grade, geographic region, parent education level, race, sex

Reliability
Internal consistency: Subtests: .71–.99
Composite(s): .86–.99

Test-Retest: Subtests: .81–.99
Composite(s): .91–.99

Interscorer: .94–.98

Validity
Content: Yes
Construct: subtest correlations, correlation with ability, correlation with achievement, group differentiation
Criterion: .21–.91

WJ III

Name:	Woodcock-Johnson III Tests of Achievement and Cognitive Abilities
Author(s):	Woodcock, R. W., McGrew, K., & Mather, N.
Publisher:	Riverside Publishing, 8420 Bryn Mawr Ave., Chicago, IL 60631-3476

Scoring Information

Subtests: *Achievement:* Letter-Word Identification, Reading Fluency, Story Recall, Understanding Directions, Calculations, Math, Fluency, Spelling, Writing Fluency, Passage Comprehension, Applied Problems, Writing Samples, Story Recall-Delayed, Word Attack, Picture Vocabulary, Oral Comprehension, Editing, Reading Vocabulary, Quantitative Concepts, Academic Knowledge, Spelling of Sounds, Sound Awareness, Punctuation and Capitalization

Cognitive Abilities: Verbal Comprehension, Visual-Auditory Learning, Spatial Relations, Sound Blending, Concept Formation, Visual Matching, Numbers Reversed, Incomplete Words, Auditory Working Memory, Visual-Auditory Learning-Delayed, General Information, Retrieval Fluency, Picture Recognition, Auditory Retention, Analysis-Synthesis, Decision Speed, Memory for Words, Rapid Picture Naming, Planning, Pair Cancellation

Composite(s): *Achievement:* Reading, Oral Language, Mathematics, Written Language, Knowledge, and Supplemental

Cognitive Abilities: Verbal Ability, Thinking Ability, Cognitive Efficiency, Supplemental

Technical Information

Standardization

Size: 8,818 subjects in more than 100 geographically diverse U.S. communities: (1,143 subjects in pre-K, 4,783 subjects in K–12, 1,165 subjects undergraduate and graduate students, 1,843 subjects adults)

Sample char.:   Census region, community size, education of adults, Hispanic, occupation of adults, occupation status of adults, race, sex, type of college/university, type of school

Reliability

Internal consistency:	Subtests:	.61–.98 (Cognitive) .41–.99 (Achievement)
	Composite(s):	.70–.99 (Cognitive) .70–.98 (Achievement)
Test-Retest:	Subtests:	.35–.98
	Composite(s):	not reported
Interscorer:	Subtests:	.71–.99
	Composite(s):	not reported

Validity

Content: Yes

Construct: factor analysis, correlations with ability, bias studies

Criterion: .65–.81

WISC-IV

Name: Wechsler Intelligence Scale for Children–Fourth Edition
Author(s): Wechsler, D.
Publisher: The Psychological Corporation, 19500 Bulverde Rd., San Antonio, TX 78259

Scoring Information

Subtests: Block Design, Similarities, Digit Span, Picture Concepts, Coding, Vocabulary, Letter-Number Sequencing, Matrix Reasoning, Comprehension, Symbol Search, Picture Completion, Cancellation, Information, Arithmetic, Word Reasoning
Composite(s): Full-Scale IQ

Technical Information

Standardization
Size: 2,200 subjects representing the four major geographic regions of the United States
Sample char.: age, geographic region, parental education level, race/ethnicity, sex

Reliability
Internal consistency: Subtests: .65.–92
Composite(s): .96–.97

Test-Retest: Subtests: .76–.92
Composite(s): .93

Interscorer: Subtests: .95–.98
Composite(s): n/a

Validity
Content: Yes
Construct: correlations with ability, correlations with achievement, composite correlations, factor analysis, subtest correlations
Criterion: Concurrent validity: .10–.80

Woodcock Reading Mastery Tests–RNU

Name: Woodcock Reading Mastery Tests–Revised, Normative Update
Author(s): Woodcock, R. W.
Publisher: American Guidance Services, 4201 Woodland Rd., Circle Pines, MN 55014

Scoring Information

Subtests: Visual-Auditory Learning, Letter Identification, Word Identification, Word Attack, Word Comprehension, Passage Comprehension
Composite(s): Basic Skills Cluster, Readiness Cluster, Reading Comprehension Cluster, Total Reading

Technical Information

Standardization
Size: 3,700 (3,184 K–12 students, 245 young adults ages 18–22) at 129 sites in 40 states
Sample char.: ethnicity, grade, parental education, race, region, sex, SES

Reliability
Internal consistency: Subtests: .68–.99
Composite(s): .54–.99

Test-Retest: Subtests: not reported
Composite(s): not reported

Validity
Content: Yes
Construct: correlation with achievement
Criterion: .35–.91

The following is a list of tests often used for identifying gifted and talented students, but were not reviewed here because their norms, if included, were collected more than 10 years ago:

California Achievement Test–5th Edition (1992)
CTB Macmillan-McGraw-Hill
20 Ryan Ranch Rd., Monterey, CA 93940

Creativity Assessment Packet (1980)
Williams, F.
PRO-ED
8700 Shoal Creek Blvd., Austin, TX 78757-6897

Creative Behavior Inventory (1989)
Kirshenbaum, R. J.
Creative Learning Press, P.O. Box 320,
Mansfield Center, CT 06250

Eby Gifted Index (1989)
Eby, J. W.
United-DOK Publishers, P.O. Box 1099, Buffalo, NY 14224

The Eby Gifted Behavior Index (1983)
Eby, J. W.
United-DOK Publishers, P.O. Box 1099, Buffalo, NY 14224

Group Inventory for Finding Creativity (GIFT, 1980)
Rimm, S. B.
Educational Assessment Service, Route One Box 139-A,
Watertown, WI 53094

Khatena Torrance Creative Perception Inventory (1976)
Torrance, P. E., & Khatena, J.
Scholastic Testing Service, 480 Meyer Rd.,
Bensenville, IL 60106-1617

Matrix Analogies Tests (1985)
Naglieri, J.
The Psychological Corporation, 19500 Bulverde Rd.,
San Antonio, TX 78259

Myers-Briggs Type Indicator (MBTI, 1985)
    Myers & McCaulley
    Consulting Psychologists Press, 577 College Ave.,
    Palo Alto, CA 94306

Murphy-Meisgeier Type Indicator for Children (1987)
    Meisgeier & Murphy
    Consulting Psychologists Press, 577 College Ave.,
    Palo Alto, CA 94306

Norris Educational Achievement Test (1992)
    Switzer & Gruber
    Western Psychological Services, 12031 Wilshire Blvd.,
    Los Angeles, CA 90025

The Rating Scale for Leadership (1986)
    Lois Roets
    407 W. Cherry, New Sharon, LA 50207

Slosson Intelligence Test for Children and Adults (1990)
    Slosson, Nicholson, & Hibpshman
    Slosson Educational Publications, P.O. Box 280,
    East Aurora, NY 14052

Stanford Achievement Test–Abbreviated (8th Edition) (1992)
    The Psychological Corporation, 19500 Bulverde Rd.,
    San Antonio, TX 78259

Publishers and Addresses

American Guidance Services
4201 Woodland Road
Circle Pines, MN 55014
(800) 328-2560

Creative Learning Press
P.O. Box 320
Mansfield, CT 06250
(800) 518-8004

CTB-Macmillan-McGraw-Hill
20 Ryan Ranch Rd.
Monterey, CA 93940
(800) 538-9547

Great Potential Press
(Previously known as Gifted Psychology Press)
P.O. Box 5057
Scottsdale, AZ 85261
(602) 954-4200

Harcourt-Brace Educational Measurement
555 Academic Ct.
San Antonio, TX 75204
(800) 211-8378

Hawthorne Educational Services
800 Gray Oak Dr.
Columbia, OH 65201
(800) 542-1673

PRO-ED
8700 Shoal Creek Blvd.
Austin, TX 78757-6897
(800) 897-3202

Prufrock Press
P.O. Box 8813
Waco, TX 76714-8813
(800) 998-2208

The Psychological Corporation
19500 Bulverde Rd.
San Antonio, TX 78259
(800) 872-1726

Riverside Publishing Company
8420 Bryn Mawr Ave.
Chicago, IL 60631-3476
(800) 323-9540

Scholastic Testing Service
480 Meyer Road
Bensenville, IL 60106-1617
(800) 642-6787

Slosson Educational Publications
P.O. Box 280
East Aurora, NY 14052
(716) 652-0930

Stoetling Co.
620 Wheat Lane
Wood Dale, IL 60191
(630) 860-9700

Western Psychological Services
12031 Wilshire Blvd.
Los Angeles, CA 90025
(800) 648-8857

CHAPTER FIVE

Making Decisions About Placement

by Susan K. Johnsen

W hen identifying gifted students, schools need to select qualitative and quantitative instruments that are technically adequate and that match gifted students' characteristics and the school district's program. Each state has specific rules that govern the types and kinds of assessments that should be used. In Texas, districts must identify students beginning in kindergarten and use a "minimum of three appropriate criteria that include both qualitative and quantitative measures . . . in languages they understand or with non-verbal based tests" (Texas Education Agency, 1996, Section 1, 1.5.2A, 1.5.4A, p. 4). These assessments must also include information from multiple sources for *each* area of giftedness served by the district (Texas Education Agency, Section 1, 1.5.1A, 1.1.5A, p. 4).

In meeting these guidelines, for example, a school district might select these five assessments for identification of students who are gifted in a specific academic area: teacher nomination, parent nomination, an intelligence test, an achievement test in the academic area, and a portfolio of work. These five assessments meet minimum standards: Quantitative and qualitative instruments are included and multiple sources—parent, teacher, and the student—are used. To be at an acceptable level, the school district will also want to make sure that the selected instruments are in a language that the students understand and that the standardized instruments have included bias studies in their technical manual.

Similar to Texas, most states rely on multiple criteria (Coleman, Gallagher, & Foster, 1994). This requirement is aligned with the Office for Civil Rights equal access concerns, which emphasize "multiple alternative referral sources" (Trice & Shannon, 2002; see Office for Civil Rights Checklist for Assessment of Gifted Programs in Appendix A.)

Multiple assessments are important for several reasons. First, no single test samples all behaviors (Salvia & Ysseldyke, 2001). Even intelligence tests vary according to theories and definitions that underlie the test design. Second, tests measuring the same trait may relate to one another, but produce different scores. For example, a student might score 130 on one intelligence test (in the very superior range) and 110 on another intelligence test (in the above-average range). Both tests may have good technical qualities, but simply sample different behaviors, be based on different definitions, be individually or group administered, or have different standard errors of measurement. Third, several sources of information (e.g., parent, teacher, student, and peers) will provide examples of behaviors across different settings and provide a broader picture of the gifted student. Gifted students may show more of their abilities at home or with friends. Coleman and Cross (2001) made the excellent point that certain behaviors are simply not exhibited in certain settings because the student doesn't have the opportunity or important others, such as friends, teachers, or parents might not understand or approve.

Richert (1991), on the other hand, has suggested that more is not always better—multiple measures can increase elitism in identification. For example, a district might choose to use grades, teacher nominations, and achievement tests, which might exclude gifted students who were underachievers, who didn't have a strong academic background, or who were gifted in other areas besides academics. *The National Report on Identification* (Alvino, McDonnel, & Richert, 1981; Richert, 1985) offered these six principles in developing a comprehensive, fair identification system:

108

- Advocacy—is it in the best interests of students?
- Defensibility—is it based on best research and recommendations?
- Equity—does it provide equal opportunity for every child?
- Pluralism—does it use the broadest definition of giftedness?

- Comprehensiveness—does it serve many gifted students?
- Pragmatism—does it allow for modification and use accessible resources?

Along with the use of multiple assessments, these principles need to be considered when districts establish an identification process.

The Identification Process

While all schools are required to identify students at least once a year (Texas Education Agency, 1996, Section 1.1.3A), some elect to identify students on an ongoing basis, referring students as they display characteristics in the classroom or in the community. Identification policies also need to address "furloughs, reassessment, exiting of students from program services, transfer students, and appeals of district decisions regarding program placement" (Texas Education Code, Chapter 89, 19 TAC §89.1[5]). Students who fit within these categories may be included in the overall identification process or may be treated on a case-by-case basis. For example, a student who transfers from another gifted program might be screened using the same identification process that is used for all students in the school district or may be placed within the program on a trial basis.

The identification process may vary. Some schools may choose to administer all of the assessments to *all* of the children at a particular grade level (e.g., kindergarten; Texas Education Agency, 1996, Section 1, 1.5.2R) and then decide which children will be referred to a final selection committee for placement into programs for gifted and talented children. Other districts may develop a three-phase process: nomination, screening, and selection (see Figure 5.1). At each of these phases, decisions must be made to determine which children progress to the next phase of assessment or placement. Some researchers suggest the addition of a validation phase in which identification procedures are evaluated by the outside (Feldhusen, Asher, & Hoover, 1984; Feldhusen & Baska, 1985; Feldhusen, Hoover, & Sayler, 1990). This step is important in assuring that the process is valid, that is, that it identifies the gifted and talented students who need services.

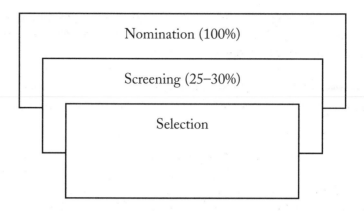

Figure 5.1 Phases in the Identification Process

Nomination

A large group of students needs to be created during the nomination phase, even those who show only vague hints of giftedness. All students who exhibit any or some of the characteristics that indicate special gifts and talents should have an *equal opportunity* to be nominated (see Office for Civil Rights Checklist for Assessment of Gifted Programs in Appendix A). The placement of students in special education programs or with certain teachers who may or may not believe in gifted education should not preclude their inclusion in the nomination group. Every effort should be made to involve students from special populations, such as those with disabilities, from minority or lower income backgrounds, with limited English proficiency, and from rurally isolated areas. School districts may want to consider placing ads in local newspapers and sending flyers home in multiple languages that advertise the program and describe the identification process to parents. Nomination instruments may include teacher and parent checklists, group intelligence and achievement tests, portfolios of work, peer and self-nominations, teacher reports of students' learning, and student background information.

If teachers are a part of the nomination process, they need to receive professional development training in the characteristics of gifted and talented students. With training, teachers identify more children (e.g., 85%) than untrained teachers (e.g., 40%; Gear, 1978). In addition, teachers at the high school level are

110

better at identifying gifted students than at the middle school or elementary years (Cornish, 1968; Jacobs, 1971; Pegnato & Birch, 1959). In fact, parents are actually better at identifying very young children (e.g., 76%) than teachers (4.3%) when using an intelligence test as the criterion (Jacobs). Once trained, teachers should observe their students when they are involved in activities that are more open-ended and require more complex thinking and other behaviors. If the tasks are not challenging and require mostly single answers or low-level responses, gifted students do not have sufficient opportunities to demonstrate their higher level abilities. Some states ensure that opportunities are provided during the nomination process by using a "prereferral" process similar to special education. In this process, the teacher uses a variety of strategies in the classroom to determine if the student might be served within the general education program or needs services beyond the classroom (see Table 5.1). Strategies relate to motivation and research, rate or pacing, preference, and content and instruction.

In all cases, the nomination instruments should be fair to the culture. Culturally appropriate measures usually a) ensure that the student understands the purpose and the nature of the testing process, b) minimize language, c) include practice items, d) minimize time constraints, and e) present novel problems instead of narrow school-related information (Jensen, 1969).

Finally, multiple sources—parents, teachers, student, and peers—need to be used in the nomination phase to ensure equal access. Unless required by the program (e.g., writing, visual and performing arts), the formats of the assessments might also vary so that all students may perform using their strengths. For example, some activities might require verbal responses; others, manipulative responses; and still others, written responses.

Screening

Once all of the nomination information is collected, the identification committee may determine which students will proceed to the second phase: screening. While many districts choose 20–25% of their population for further screening, others may choose to administer all of the screening measures to the entire school population or to all students who are nominated for the

111

Table 5.1

Prereferral Strategies

Motivation and Research	Rate or Pacing	Preference	Content and Instruction
1. Establish system for long-range assignments.	1. Provide fewer drill and practice activities when material is learned.	1. Arrange for a mentor to work with student in interest area or area of greatest strength.	1. Provide opportunities for students to express and elaborate on thoughts and ideas through interactive dialogues; discussion.
2. Provide opportunities for open-ended, self-directed activities.	2. Provide opportunities for students to demonstrate mastery of skills and concepts.	2. Vary the method of presentation with lecture, small groups, large group, demonstrations, individual experimentation.	2. Use advanced supplementary materials.
3. Use contracts.	3. Give a pretest and if the student knows the materials, proceed to the next unit or chapter.	3. Give students choices of activities in learning the content.	4. Provide opportunities for development of creativity.
4. Provide instruction in research skills needed to conduct an independent study in student's interest area.	4. Cluster group by academic strengths.		5. Ask higher-level questions.
5. Provide independent learning activities.	5. Provide self-checking materials.		6. Provide tests at a higher level of thinking.
			7. Provide materials that emphasize "depth" or "breadth" in a specific subject area.

program. No one instrument should be used as a single criterion. For example, movement to the screening phase should not be based on a cut-off score from a single measure, such as the 85th percentile on an achievement test or a single teacher nomination; rather, it should be based on successful performance on several assessments used during the nomination phase. These assessments might include parent, teacher, self, or peer checklists or observations; schoolwork that is a part of a portfolio; and achievement or aptitude tests. In this phase, the committee will want to include all students who appear to exhibit or have the potential to exhibit the desired qualities. A good rule of thumb might be when in doubt, screen the student further.

During the screening phase, additional information is collected on the nominated students. Since the number of students in the screening phase will be smaller than in the nomination phase, a district might consider using individually administered measures or methods that allow for more clinical observations such as interviews, participation in a classroom for gifted students, or observations of the ways in which the student learns new information (e.g., dynamic assessment). Dynamic assessment focuses on the interaction between the gifted student and the task. The tasks should be problem-based and require complex strategies that discriminate among intelligent individuals (Geary & Brown, 1991; Kurtz & Weinert, 1989; Scruggs & Mastropieri, 1985). These novel tasks might provide opportunities for varying rates of learning, efficiency in retrieving information for solving problems, transfer to new tasks, and knowledge about a learner's strategies (Johnsen, 1997). Again, all students should have opportunities to demonstrate their best performance levels. By the end of the nomination and screening phases, a school should have data from multiple sources and quantitative and qualitative assessments.

Selection

During the selection phase, the identification committee examines all of the data that have been collected on each child nominated and screened. The committee should be comprised of "at least three local district or campus educators who have received training in the nature and needs of gifted students"

(Texas Education Agency, 1996, Section 1, 1.7A; 19 TAC §89.1[4]). *All* data from both the nomination and screening phases should be considered. To ensure objectivity, the committee may initially want to identify students by number only and add clinical or qualitative information later.

The identification committee determines which students are selected for which gifted program. While many districts may select 5–10% of their student population, this percentage will vary depending upon the number of programs provided for gifted and talented students and the number of students whose characteristics indicate the need for services that are not ordinarily provided by the school. Given the synthesis of the qualitative and quantitative information, the committee might also want to create a differentiation plan that includes specific programming based on the gifted student's strengths and weaknesses, long- and short-term goals, classroom activities within the gifted and the general education program, and evaluation. These plans will set the stage for the next phase, which includes an annual evaluation of the identification procedure (Texas Education Agency, 1996, Section 5, 5.3A; TEC §§11.251-11.253).

Evaluation and Modification

The following questions might be used to guide the school district in building a defensible procedure for identifying gifted and talented students:

1. Is the procedure based on best research and recommendations?
2. Does it match the district's definition and program options?
3. Do all students have an equal opportunity to be nominated?
4. Are special populations considered in the nomination process?
5. Are all students able to demonstrate their strengths?
6. Are assessments fair to student cultures?
7. Are all students able to demonstrate their abilities in classroom activities?
8. Are multiple sources of information used?

9. Are all data considered during the selection phase?
10. Are the students' data evaluated objectively?
11. Are all students who need a differentiated education being identified?
12. Do identified students perform well in the program that matches their gifts or talents?

The school district will want to continue collecting data to ensure that all gifted students are being served effectively. Data from the identification process may be correlated with future performance in the classroom, future performance on other assessments, future performance on assessments used for program evaluation purposes, and future performance in out-of-school settings.

Appeals and Due Process

Under the Fifth and Fourteenth Amendments or by state or federal statutes, due process procedures are imposed on school districts (Karnes & Marquardt, 1991). In 10 states, gifted students are afforded the same provisions as handicapped students. Other states, including Texas, have general due process procedures that are applicable to the gifted (Karnes & Marquardt).

To assure due process rights, a school district will want to identify clearly for parents and guardians time frames and steps in a locally developed appeals process (Texas Education Agency, 1996, Section 1, 1.2A, 1.2.6R; 19 TAC §89.1[5]). These steps may include meaningful parent meetings with (a) teachers, (b) the selection committee or building administrator, (c) a school district committee that would include the director or administrator responsible for the gifted program, and, finally, (d) the school board. If these meetings do not resolve the issues, the school district may want to bring in an impartial and professionally trained mediator. The mediator would discuss the important issues with the involved participants and try to resolve any remaining conflicts. If these conflicts are still not resolved, the parents or the school district may contact the state education agency and initiate a formal hearing. Hearing procedures generally allow parents to choose if the hearing is open or closed and if their child may attend. Both sides may choose to have counsel and present expert witnesses. If the formal hearing still does not resolve the conflicts,

115

the parents or the school district may still choose to litigate in the federal or state court system. "Litigation should be the last resort . . . going to court is expensive, time consuming, adversarial, and emotionally draining" (Karnes & Marquardt, 1991, p. 37).

Organizing Data for Decision Making

At each phase in the identification process, the committee needs to examine qualitative and quantitative information. These data may be organized in a variety of ways: case studies, profiles, matrices, or other forms. Whichever approach is used, the identification committee should follow these guidelines.

Guideline 1: Weighting of assessments. If each assessment has equal reliability and validity for identifying gifted and talented students, then each should have equal value in the decision-making process. The committee should not assign more weight or importance to one assessment over another. Following are five examples of "weighting," each of which is inappropriate.

1. A single source (e.g., teacher nomination) or a cut-off score on a single test (e.g., 85th percentile on an achievement test) is used to nominate a student for the gifted program. This approach weights the instrument or the test in the overall identification process. Remember that untrained teachers may not refer economically disadvantaged children or tend to nominate students who are like themselves (Peterson & Margolin, 1997).
2. Quantitative measures such as norm-referenced intelligence or achievement tests may be assigned more influence in the selection of students than qualitative measures such as product scores, parent nominations, or performance in informal lessons because the former are judged to be more accurate or reliable than the latter.
3. Certain tests are assigned more points. Scores on an intelligence test might earn more points than a teacher nomination or teacher nominations might earn more points than parent nominations.
4. A single source (e.g., a teacher) provides the majority of the qualitative information such as grades, checklists, and

product scores. One teacher's ratings might be weighted three times as much as any other source of information.

5. Several subtests and the composite score that assess the same trait (e.g., achievement) are used from the same measure and counted each time. This means that a single measure receives a multiplied weight.

In summary, no one assessment or source of information should carry more weight than another. In selecting and designing a form, the committee will want to ensure that all assessments receive equal weight.

Guideline 2: Comparable scores. The committee may receive scores in various forms. These scores might include raw scores, percentiles, stanine scores, and standard scores. To interpret the different test scores, the committee needs to know (a) how they compare to one another and (b) what reference population or norm group is represented.

Raw scores that represent the total number of points a student earns on a checklist, a test, or a rating form are not interpretable until they have been converted to a standardized scoring system. Standard scores have an advantage over other types of scores because the measurement units are equal and can be averaged or manipulated (Feldhusen, Baska, & Womble, 1981).

Using the raw scores, the committee can determine standard scores by following the directions in Appendix B, "Converting Raw Scores to Standard Scores." Once the raw scores have been converted to standard scores, comparisons may be made with other scores by using a conversion chart.

Test manuals and publishers provide conversion charts that compare various test scores with one another and to a normal distribution (e.g., the bell-shaped curve). For example, you will note in Table 5.2 that a performance at two standard deviations (SD) above the mean (M) represents a score that may be interpreted in these ways:

- The score is at the 98th percentile.
- The score is at the ninth stanine.
- The standard score is 130 (with a mean of 100 and standard deviation of 15).

- The student performed better than 98% of the students who took the test.
- The student is performing in the superior to very superior ranges.

A score in the superior range or at the 95th percentile is comparable to a score at the eighth stanine and to a standard score of 124. (Note that age- and grade-equivalent scores are not represented since they are difficult to interpret and should not be used when comparing scores.)

The committee also needs to know what reference population or norm group is represented by the score. For example, when raw scores were converted to percentiles, were the students at all ability levels represented or only those nominated? If only the nomination pool scores were converted, the students would be compared with only a small percentage of the local population. On the other hand, if all students at a particular grade level were included, students would be compared with their entire local population. A student's score will be higher when compared to all students his or her age and will be lower when compared only with students nominated for the gifted and talented program.

Local norms are also different from national norms. Unless the school system's population is representative of the nation as a whole, local norms are likely to be different in some ways from the population on which a test was standardized. For example, more students may be from minority backgrounds or from middle or upper income levels than the national average. Therefore, it is important to consider the reference group when interpreting scores (Mills, Ablard, & Brody, 1993). As noted above, students whose scores are compared with a local nomination group may not appear to perform as well as when their scores are compared to an entire local population. In a similar fashion, students compared with a national gifted population may not appear to perform as well as when their scores are compared to an entire national population. Similarly, young kindergarten children who have summer birthdays may appear to do less well than older children from the same grade level. In summarizing data, the committee will want to ensure the scores are comparable and the reference groups are clearly understood.

Table 5.2

Relationships of Various Standard Scores
to Percentile Ranks and Descriptions

Distance From Mean	Description (% of pop.)	Percentile Ranks	Standard Scores		Stanines (% of pop.)
			Dev. IQ	Z Score	
+3*SD*		99.9	150.0	3.3	
		99.9	145.0	3.0	
		99.8	143.5	2.9	
		99.7	142.0	2.8	
	Very Superior (2.34%)	99.6	140.5	2.7	
		99.5	140.0	2.7	
		99.5	139.0	2.6	
		99.4	137.5	2.5	
		99.2	136.0	2.4	9 (4%)
		99	135.0	2.3	
		99	134.5	2.3	
		99	133.0	2.2	
		98	131.5	2.1	
+2*SD*		98	130.0	2.0	
		97	128.5	1.9	
		96	127.0	1.8	
	Superior (6.87%)	96	125.5	1.7	
		96	125.0	1.7	
		95	124.0	1.6	
		93	122.5	1.5	
		92	121.0	1.4	8 (7%)
		91	120.0	1.3	
		90	119.5	1.3	
	Above-Average (16.12%)	88	118.0	1.2	
+1*SD*		86	116.5	1.1	
		84	115.0	1.0	7 (12%)
		82	113.5	.9	
		79	112.0	.8	
		76	110.5	.7	
	Average (49.51%)	75	110.0	.7	
		73	109.0	.6	
		69	107.5	.5	6 (17%)
		66	106.0	.4	
		63	105.0	.3	
		62	104.5	.3	
		58	103.0	.2	
Mean		54	101.5	.1	
		50	100.0	0	
		46	98.5	-.1	
		42	97.0	-.2	5 (20%)
		38	95.5	-.3	
		37	95.0	-.3	

119

Guideline 3: Error in measures. Every measure contains a certain amount of error. This error is estimated through the standard error of measurement. Depending on the measure's reliability and standard deviation, the size of this error will vary across grade or age levels, across subtests, and between different tests. No single test score number should be construed as "the one true score." A student's true score will lie somewhere within a range of scores established by the standard error of measurement.

For example, suppose that David scores 120 on an intelligence test and the standard error of measurement (*SEM*) is 5 points. The interpreter of this score might say that 68% of the time David will score between 115 and 125 (plus 5 and minus 5 = one standard error of measurement); that 95% of the time David will score between 110 and 130 (plus 10 and minus 10 = two standard errors of measurement); and that 99% of the time David will score between 107 and 133 (plus 13 and minus 13 = 2.6 standard errors of measurement). (See Table 5.3 for additional standard errors of measurement.) Test manuals should report the standard error of measurement for each age or grade level or both. While more qualitative measures may not have a calculated standard error, the committee always should consider that some error is inherent in all methods and procedures that are used (see Appendix B for "Calculating the Standard Error of Measurement").

Guideline 4. Best performance reported. Estimates of student potential come from their best performance. Attempts to compress all performance data into a single number to use as a cut-off score for entry into the gifted program can be misleading when student performance shows considerable variability. Student scores may actually range from the very superior level to the average level within one measure or across measures; a compressed single score is less likely to reveal these ranges. Committee members need to see the peaks and valleys in student performance. The committee should consider the student's highest performance as indicative of his or her potential. The highest score is most often the truest (Tolan, 1992a, 1992b).

Guideline 5. Description of the student. While numbers are helpful in comparing certain kinds of data, not all information about the student can be described numerically. Therefore, space

Table 5.3

Confidence Levels for Different Standard Errors of Measurement

Confidence Level	Band of Error
68%	± 1 SEM
85%	± 1.44 SEMs
90%	± 1.645 SEMs
95%	± 1.96 SEMs
99%	± 2.576 SEMs

should be provided for anecdotal information or clinical observations (e.g., how he or she acquires new information and uses reasoning strategies). This qualitative information may be especially useful when attempting to match instructional strategies to student characteristics.

In summary, these five guidelines can be used in designing or selecting a form or process to organize multiple kinds of data. To evaluate a form or process under consideration, district staff could ask the following questions based on these guidelines:

1. Do all assessments receive equal weight or value?
2. Are the scores comparable?
3. Are errors in measures considered?
4. Does the form or process provide the opportunity for the identification committee to examine each student's best performance?
5. Does the form or process allow the committee to consider anecdotal and other descriptive information?

Sample Forms and Procedures

Many possible forms and procedures meet the above guidelines. Each must (a) be based on best research and recommendations, (b) relate to the school's definition and program, (c) use qualitative and quantitative assessments, (d) use multiple sources, and (e) be unbiased. Feldhusen and Baska (1985) cautioned against using forms that *combine* assessment data, particularly matrices. Borland (1989) suggested that matrices do more harm than good by adding disparate subscale scores from a variety of qualitative and quantitative instruments. The next section of this chapter therefore provides a few forms and procedures that a committee might use in organizing data to identify gifted and talented students.

Case Study

Borland and Wright (1994) suggested that a case study approach is the best way to identify children from lower socioeconomic backgrounds. A case study provides more depth, shows growth of performance over time, and incorporates evidence from a variety of sources and settings. Clark (1997) suggested that a case study might include nomination forms, teacher reports of student functioning, family history and student background, peer identification, student inventory of interests, student work and achievements, student and parent interviews, and a variety of test protocols (intelligence, achievement, and creativity).

The cover page from a folder of evidence is included in Figure 5.2. At the top of the page is student demographic information. Note that the date of birth is included and is particularly important in the primary grades. Quantitative information is separated from qualitative information. In this case, the school district has set minimum stanine scores of two 8s and one 9 for the quantitative, but not for the qualitative information. The committee reviews each of these qualitative assessments using characteristics of gifted and talented students, product or performance rubrics, or both. Each piece of evidence is scored as meeting or not meeting the criteria. These criteria may be established for individual assessments or for the case study as a whole.

In the example, Edward Ochoa scored 135 on the Reasoning subtest of the Screening Assessment for Gifted Elementary Students or the ninth stanine (see Figure 5.2). He also scored at the 95th percentile, the eighth stanine, on the Math subtest of the Iowa Test of Basic Skills and is making grades in the 90s in math, science, and social studies. While the teacher's appraisal was negative, he had a strong portfolio, which showed his mathematical

Decisions About Placement

Student: *Edward Ochoa*   D.O.B.:   *10-31-93*   ID#: *75-4253*
Parents: *Luisa & Manuel Ochoa*   Phone (H): *723-5604*   (W): *712-6489*
Address: *516 North Main*   City: *Hometown* Zip: *75689*
Home School/Grade: *Sunshine/Grade 5*   Date of Review: *5/14/03*

Quantitative Indicators (Min. stanines: two 8s and one 9)   Criterion Met
_____

Achievement Testing
Test Name: *Iowa Test of Basic Skills*   Date: *2/10/03*
  Reading: *84th Percentile*   *(7th stanine)*   Yes   **(No)**
  Math: *95th Percentile*   *(8th stanine)*   **(Yes)**   No
  Language: *90th Percentile*   *(8th stanine)*   **(Yes)**   No

Other Tests (Name):   Date: Yes   No

Report Card:
  88   *88*   *94*   *99*   *90*   **(Yes)**   No
  Reading   LA   Math   Science   SS

Aptitude/Intelligence Testing
SAGES-2 Scores: *Reasoning—135 (9th stanine)* Date: *3/12/03*   **(Yes)**   No

Other Tests (Name):   Date: Yes   No

Qualitative Indicators

Observations
Teacher: *with reservation about maturity*   Date: *4/07/03*   Yes   **(No)**
Parent: *highly recommends*   Date: *3/21/03*   **(Yes)**   No
Other: *counselor recommends*   Date: **(Yes)**   No

Performance/Products
Portfolio Items: *writing, math reasoning*   Date: *3/30/03*   **(Yes)**   No
Other: Date: Yes   No

Interviews
Student: Date: Yes   No
Parent: *Discovery channel/collections*   Date: *4/15/03*   **(Yes)**   No
Other: *Peer: original and impatient*   Date: *4/20/03*   **(Yes)**   No

Committee Decision

After reviewing the information, the committee agrees that *Edward Ochoa*
Qualifies √   Does not Qualify   Is Provisionally Placed
in the gifted education program.

123

Figure 5.2 Case Study Form

_____

Note. Adapted from the Carrollton-Farmers Branch School District, 1997.

reasoning and creative writing ability. He was rated outstanding in "depth of knowledge expressed," "ability to see relationships and connections," and "age and developmental appropriateness of product." His peers and parent interviews also showed evidence of many characteristics of gifted and talented students. The counselor added, "Some have described Edward's creative writing assignments as truly creative; his teacher sees them as strange. His peers see him as original, anxious to try new things, and impatient. At home, he likes to watch the Discovery Channel." Overall, the committee agreed that Edward Ochoa had sufficient evidence for his placement in the school district's program. Now, review the case study form using the criteria suggested earlier in this chapter:

1. *Are the data from some measures more important than others?* No, the committee considered quantitative and qualitative information as equally important. Information was acquired from quantitative (e.g., achievement and aptitude testing) and qualitative (e.g., observations, student performance, surveys, and interviews) sources.

2. *Are the scores comparable?* Broad bands of performance (e.g., stanines) were used to compare the objective indicators. Quantitative scores were not combined with one another or with the subjective indicators. After establishing interrater reliability, the trained committee discussed and rated each of the assessments for each of the nominated students.

3. *Is the error in tests considered?* Yes. Broad bands of performance were used instead of single test scores.

4. *Does the form provide an opportunity for the identification committee to examine the student's best performance?* Definitely. Scores were listed separately for each quantitative instrument. The committee also reviewed each piece of qualitative evidence in Edward's folder, including checklists, products, and anecdotal summaries.

5. *Does the form provide a space for additional comments or anecdotal information?* Definitely. A variety of individuals have described Edward's performance—teachers, parents, peers, and himself.

Profile

The profile form in Figure 5.3 represents a way to display student data. In the upper left corner, student demographic characteristics (e.g., name, age, date of birth, gender, and school) are included. On the left side of the form, the district lists the measures used in the nomination and screening phases. These assessments match both local student and program characteristics within one district. The selection of these assessments most likely will vary depending on the district's student population and program characteristics.

In the upper right corner, the district lists scores that are comparable to one another. For example, line C relates all scores to a normal curve, line B to percentile scores, and line A to ranges of performance. By reading the scores from bottom to top, one can see that a mean score is comparable to the 50th percentile and comparable to a score in the average range. In like manner, a score at or above plus two standard deviations (+2 SD) is comparable to the 98th percentile and scores in the superior to very superior ranges. Additional lines of comparable scores may be added by your district.

In the example, to the right of the measures is the profile area where individual student data are recorded. Since the district wants to identify the top 5% of its population, a district line has been drawn at the 95th percentile. The district's students who have at least three strengths are selected for its gifted program. This is indicated by scores to the right of the district line. Each district should decide where to place its line. Districts that raise the line above the 95th percentile may encounter problems since more test error is found above this range.

On the completed profile form, you will note in number 1, Product/Performance, out of a possible 8 points, Sarah's six products from her academic portfolio earned an average of 6 points. Since only 8% of the local population achieved within this range, this score placed her in the superior range, with a standard score of 121 (M = 100, SD = 15; see Table 5.2). A standard error of measurement (1 SEM) of 4 points was calculated (see Appendix B). To achieve the 68% confidence level, 4 points (1 SEM) were added and subtracted to Sarah's score (refer to Table 5.3). Sarah's score now fell within the 117–125 range or within the above-average to superior ranges.

Name: *Sarah Francine* ID#: *6783* School: *Washington* Teacher: *Nolen* Grade: *3* D.O.B: *5/6/95*	Poor	Below Average	Average	Above Avergae	Superior	Very Superior	A
Parents: *Sally Francine* Address: *325 Overview #5* Phone: *678-3921* (H);	%0 2 8 16 25 50 70 84 91 98 99.9						B
698-1209 (W) Date of Review: *1/31/04*	-2sd -1sd *M* +1sd +2sd +3sd +4sd						C

1. Products/Performance Raw score: 6/8 points SS: 121 (92%ile)						L				
2. Teacher Checklist *Renzulli Motivation* Raw score: 20 points SS: 110 (75%ile)					L	District Line				
3. Parent Checklist Raw score: 30 points SS: 127 (96%ile)						L				
4. Achievement Test *California Achievement Test* SS: 119 (90%ile)										
5. Intelligence Test *WISC III* SS: 130										

Comments and Recommendation:
Sarah really enjoys those activities that require more complex thinking.
When she becomes involved in a project, she doesn't want to stop and
return to her class work. The committee believes that she should be placed
in the gifted program.

Figure 5.3 Profile Form

Note. Adapted from the gifted and talented program, Lubbock Independent School District, 1989.

Sarah received a raw score of 20 points on the Renzulli teacher nomination checklist. When this raw score was converted to a standard score, Sarah's score was .7 above the mean, 110, at the 75th percentile or in the average range. Again, a standard error of measurement (one *SEM*) of 5 points was calculated (see Appendix B). At the 68% confidence level, Sarah's score fell within the 105–115 range or within the average to above-average range.

Sarah received a raw score of 30 points on a locally prepared parent nomination checklist. When this raw score was converted to a standard score, Sarah's score was 1.8 above the mean, 127, at the 96th percentile or in the superior range. A standard error of measurement (one *SEM*) of 4 points was calculated. At the 68% confidence level, Sarah's score fell within the 123–131 range or within the superior to very superior range.

She performed better than 90% of the students on the total battery of the California Achievement Test (CAT) with a 119 standard score. At the 68% confidence level, one *SEM* was added and subtracted to the standard score. Sarah's score fell within the above-average to superior ranges, 114–124, or from the 83rd to the 95th percentile.

Finally, on the Wechsler Intelligence Scale for Children–Third Edition, Sarah obtained a full-scale intelligence quotient of 130 (i.e., mean of 100 with a standard deviation of 15). Given a 3-point standard error of measurement, 3 points were added and subtracted to Sarah's score of 130 to achieve an 8% confidence level. Sarah's score fell within the superior to very superior ranges or from 127 to 133.

Because Sarah obtained four scores at or to the right of the district line drawn at the 95th percentile, the committee recommended that she be included in the program. Now, review the completed profile form using the criteria suggested earlier in this chapter:

1. *Are the data from some measures more important than others?*
   No, all measures were considered to be equally important. Information was acquired from quantitative (e.g., the CAT and the WISC III) and qualitative (e.g., teacher and parent checklists and student product) sources. Student products were judged by the identification committee

instead of the teacher to add an additional source of information and to avoid assigning a double weight to the teacher's perceptions.

2. *Are the scores comparable?* Yes the percentiles are comparable to bands of performance that were established within the normal curve distribution (e.g., means and standard deviations). All district raw scores were converted to standard scores and then to percentiles, or to broad bands of performance. These scores were represented by "L" to indicate that local norms were used.

3. *Is the error in tests considered?* Yes. In an attempt to achieve the 68% confidence level, one standard error of measurement was added and subtracted to each student's score and all scores were reported within broad bands of performance such as average, above-average, superior, and very superior.

4. *Does the form provide an opportunity for the identification committee to examine Sarah's best performance?* Yes. Scores were not summed to obtain a cut-off score for entry into the program. The committee was able to examine Sarah's strengths and weaknesses. In this example, Sarah's relative strength was in her performance on the intelligence measure.

5. *Does the form provide a space for additional comments or anecdotal information?* Yes. The bottom of the form provided some space for these comments. Other anecdotal information could be attached to the profile form.

Minimum Scores

Another form for organizing data is the minimum scores approach. A minimum scores form with sample data is shown in Figure 5.4. At the top of the form, student demographic characteristics are included (e.g., name, age, gender, and school). On the left side of the form, the district again lists the measures used in the nomination and screening phases.

To the right of the measure's name is a column in which the *SEM* is written. The next column contains the minimum score. This minimum score corresponds to the district line on the profile. The major difference between the profile form and the min-

Identification Number: *6783*
Name: *Sarah Francine*
School: *Washington*
Parents/Guardian: *Sally Francine*
Phone: *678-3921 (H); 698-1209 (W)*

Recommended for Placement: **Yes** No
Date of Birth: *May 6, 1995*
Teacher/Grade: *Nolen / Grade 3*
Address: *325 Overview, #5*
Date of Review: *January 31, 2004*

Instruments	SEM	Minimum Score	Actual Score	+/−	Comments
Aptitude WISC III	3	121	130	+	Strong across all subtests
Achievement CAT	5	119	119	+	Strong in most areas except language
Motivation Renzulli	5	119	110	−	Sarah needs to complete more of her class work
Parent Checklist	4	120	127	+	Enjoys working by herself on projects
Products	4	120	121	+	Enjoys working with 3-D designs

Comments:
Sarah enjoys those activities that require more complex thinking. When she becomes involved in a project, she doesn't want to stop and return to her class work.

Figure 5.4 Minimum Scores Form

imum score form is that the standard error of measurement has been subtracted from the district-determined standard scores (i.e., the minimum score). On the profile form, standard errors of measurement are added and subtracted to each individual student's score and the range of scores are then plotted on the graph. In the minimum scores approach, this calculation is figured for each individual measure before the student's standard scores are recorded. In this way, the student is given an advantage of one or more standard errors of measurement. All measures must have the *SEM* subtracted.

For example, a district decides to select students for its gifted program who perform at or above the 95th percentile on three of five different measures. The 95th percentile corresponds to a standard score of 124. If a district wants to achieve a 68% confidence level, the committee will subtract approximately one standard error of measurement from the district determined minimum score (e.g., 124). If a measure has a 3-point standard error of measurement and the district wanted a 68% confidence level, the identification committee would subtract 3 points (i.e., one *SEM*) from 124 (i.e., 95th percentile or district line) and set the minimum entry score at 121, rather than 124.

The person who tallies the actual scores compares them to the minimum entry score. Students with scores at or beyond this minimum entry score receive a plus (+). If not at or beyond the minimum entry score, students receive a minus (-). Students who receive three plus marks are considered eligible for placement into the gifted program.

To use the minimum scores approach, consider Sarah's scores again (see sample completed minimum scores approach). On the WISC III, 3 points (i.e., one *SEM*) were subtracted from 124 (i.e., the 95th percentile), making the minimum score 121. Since Sarah obtained a full-scale intelligence quotient of 130, she received another plus (+) in this category.

For the California Achievement Test, the district used the 95th percentile as a cut-off score or 124 standard score ($M = 100$, $SD = 15$). Considering the 68% confidence level and one *SEM* of 5 points, the minimum score is 119 (i.e., 124 - 5 = 119). Sarah scored exactly at this level and received a plus (+) in this category.

For the Renzulli Motivational Scale, the district converted the raw scores to standard scores and found that a raw score of 27 places a student in the superior range or at a standard score of 124. A standard error of measurement of 5 points was calculated. The 5 points were subtracted from 124 to achieve a 68% confidence level, and 119 was entered in the minimum entry score column. Since Sarah received 20 points, this translated into a standard score of 110. Thus, she did not meet the minimum entry score and received a minus (-) in this category.

For the locally developed parent nomination checklist, the district converted the raw scores to standard scores and found that a raw score of 27 places a student in the superior range or at a standard score of 124. A standard error of measurement of 4 points was calculated. The 4 points were subtracted from 124 to achieve a 68% confidence level, and 120 was entered in the minimum entry score column. Since Sarah received 30 points, this translated into a standard score of 127. Thus, she met the minimum entry score and received a plus (+) in this category.

Finally, the minimum entry score for products is 120. The score was derived by subtracting 4 points, 1 *SEM* from 124, the 95th percentile or the district cut-off line. Since Sarah's score was 121, she would receive a plus (+) in this category.

In examining this minimum scores form, it is easy to see that Sarah received four plus marks and would be recommended for placement in the program for the gifted. Again, all guidelines were met: no weighting of measures occurred, the scores were comparable, error was calculated before the score was placed in the minimum entry score column, best performance could be noted, and space was provided for additional comments.

In summary, this chapter has recommended some forms that the district might use in the nomination screening and selection phases. A school will want to collect evaluation data on those who perform successfully in the program, those who don't, and those who perform somewhere in-between. A district will then want to examine relationships between categories of youngsters and the measures it uses in selection processes. An ongoing evaluation process will be well worth a district's efforts in finding those students who truly need and can benefit from a differentiated curriculum to reach their full potential.

CHAPTER SIX

Evaluating the Effectiveness of Identification Procedures

by Susan K. Johnsen

E valuation is the process that is used to determine the worth or merit of whatever is being evaluated. The evaluator uses standards to examine the value, quality, usefulness, effectiveness or significance of, in this case, the identification procedure. The evaluator then collects information that is relevant to the purpose of the evaluation and makes recommendations.

These evaluation standards have essentially been outlined in Texas by the Division of Advanced Academic Services of the Texas Education Agency (TEA). The TEA asks that schools "ensure that student assessment and services comply with accountability standards included in the Texas State Plan for the Gifted/Talented" and that this evaluation be conducted at least annually for "program improvement and development" (see standards 2.6A, 2.6.1R, and 2.6.1E, Texas Education Agency, 1996). Therefore, once the identification procedure has been outlined, the school district will want to begin the process of evaluating it immediately. While this evaluation may occur internally, it is often better to have an "outsider" who brings credibility and objectivity to the process. This chapter will discuss six components of this evaluation: the key features, data sources and instrument review, methods and measurement options, data interpretation, the report, and recommendations.

Key Features

The first step in beginning the evaluation is to select the key features of the identification procedure that might be evaluated. Some of the following key features might be selected from the state standards, specific components of the district's identification plan, or both:

1. Are families and staff aware of the identification procedures and related services for gifted and talented students? (Standard 1.1, TEA, 1996)
2. Are there policies that relate to furloughs, reassessment, exiting of students, transfer of students, and appeals of district decisions? What are the effects of these policies? (Standard 1.2, TEA, 1996)
3. Do assessment instruments match student characteristics and program services? (Standard 1.5, TEA, 1996)
4. Are the qualitative and quantitative assessments technically adequate? Are they effective in identifying students who perform well in the program? (Standard 1.5, TEA, 1996)
5. Do all students in grades K–12 have equal access to the nomination process, including students from special populations? (Standard 1.6, TEA, 1996)
6. Does the population in the district's gifted and talented program reflect the total district population? (Standard 1.6, TEA, 1996)
7. Is the procedure for selecting students valid, reliable, and statistically sound?
8. Have staff who are involved in the identification process received adequate professional development in nominating, screening, and selecting gifted and talented students? (Standards 1.7, 4.3, TEA, 1996)
9. Do identified students benefit from the program? Are all students who might benefit from the program being identified?

A district might develop a timeline for evaluating different features. For example, during the first year, the district might evaluate identification policies and whether or not assessment instruments match student characteristics and program services, while the effects of the identification procedure, such as representation and student benefits, might be evaluated in later years.

Data Sources and Instrument Review

After the key features have been identified, the school district needs to decide what types of information are needed, what instruments and sources will provide this information, and when the information will be collected. Types of information might include product ratings, logs, identification summary forms, lesson plans, observation instruments, interviews, attitude and interest inventories, rating scales, norm-referenced tests, work samples, criterion referenced tests, principal's incident reports, questionnaires and surveys, portfolios, and tapes. These types of information may be gathered from many sources, including students, teachers, parents, administrators, school board members, and other community members.

For example, to evaluate if students benefit from the program, the district will first want to describe the type of "benefit." If the benefit is academic, then the district may want to gather information from norm-referenced achievement tests that have adequate ceilings, student portfolios of work, teacher ratings of classroom performance, observations of students performing in the classroom, school district data related to SAT and AP scores, and even admission or performance in higher education settings. This information needs to be collected on an annual basis to determine student growth from year to year and the overall effectiveness of the program (e.g., gains in achievement of gifted students who participate in the program, SAT and AP scores).

Instruments will need to be reviewed according to their technical adequacy as previously described in Chapters Two, Three, and Four. It is particularly important that newly designed instruments be field-tested before being distributed district- or communitywide. In this way, the district ensures that the information collected relates to the key features that are being evaluated.

135

Methods and Assessment Options

Once the instruments and data sources are selected for a particular key feature, the next step is to identify how the data will be collected, how it will be measured, and how it will be quantified or qualitatively described or both. For example, in Table 6.1, the key feature is student academic benefit. The district decided to collect achievement tests, SAT tests, student portfolios, ratings of performance and classroom observations from students, teachers, district files, and an outside evaluator. These assessments include quantitative data (e.g., tests, ratings, and classroom observations) and qualitative data (e.g., portfolios, ratings, and classroom observations). You will notice that some of the types of information have both qualitative or descriptive components *and* quantitative or numerical components. The district wanted research methods that compared performance on tests from one year to the next to determine student academic growth. They also wanted to discover if the students who participated in the program did better on the SAT tests than those who did not participate. They wanted to look at a variety of relationships. What is the relationship between teacher ratings and performance in the classroom? What is the relationship between teacher ratings and achievement tests? What is the relationship between achievement tests and performance in the classroom? Finally, they also wanted to collect information that *described* students' work samples and their performance and interactions in the classroom.

Data Interpretation

At this stage, those involved in the evaluation will analyze the data by using statistics for the quantitative data and examining patterns and themes for the qualitative data. Sometimes, descriptive statistics—identifying the mean, median, mode—are all that are required. Other times, more sophisticated statistics might be needed to examine differences between groups of students (e.g., T-tests or Analysis of Variance or Covariance, etc.) or relationships between past and future performance (e.g., regression, discriminant analysis, etc.). If a school district doesn't have a research and evaluation division, they might want to collaborate with

Table 6.1

Type of Information, Source, Method, and Measurement of One Key Feature

Key Feature: Student Academic Benefit

Type of Information	Source	Method	Assessment
Achievement tests (ITBS, AP)	Student and district	Compare performance on tests from one year to the next.	Quantitative
SAT tests	Student and district	Mean comparisons across years of students who participate and who do not participate in the program.	Quantitative
Portfolios	Student and teacher	Description of products using the state performance criteria.	Qualitative
Ratings and summaries of performance	Teacher	Relationship between performance and achievement tests; description of performance in classroom.	Quantitative and qualitative
Observations of students	Outside evaluator	Relationship between performance, teacher ratings and achievement tests; description of interactions in the classroom.	Quantitative and qualitative

another school district's research division, a university evaluation center, or an evaluation consultant. However, quite a bit of interesting data can be gleaned from qualitative approaches. For example, do the overall products in the portfolio improve from grade to grade? How are perceptions about the identification of gifted and talented students similar across different groups of participants, stakeholders, or both? How are social interactions different in classrooms that have only gifted and talented students from a more heterogeneous setting?

Evaluators need to exercise caution in interpreting data. They need to make sure that they have a representative sample of the feature that is being evaluated. For example, did the evaluator receive responses from parents whose children were in classrooms at all grade levels and from all ethnic groups? The data also need to represent what is really happening in the identification procedure. To ensure this type of validity, the evaluator should ask others such as teachers, coordinators, parents, and students for verification of the information that has been received. The report may be written only after the evaluator determines that the data are representative of the key feature and that those involved agree with the interpretations of the data.

Report

Before writing the final report, the evaluator needs to consider the audience and the original purpose for the evaluation. What did the audience want to learn about the identification procedure? How might the report be written so that the audience understands its strengths and weaknesses? What recommendations will be helpful in improving the identification procedure? Generally the report has six sections:

1. The first section is the executive summary, which provides a brief overview of the evaluation for people who are too busy to read the entire report. It must include a synopsis of each of the other sections.
2. The second section includes background information about, in this case, the identification procedure. The background might include school district policies and

descriptive information about the identification procedure, the type of services that are provided for identified students, the personnel who are involved in the identification process, and the students who participate in the current program.

3. The third section describes the evaluation study itself: the purpose, the key features and questions, data sources and instruments, methods and assessment options, and data analysis.

4. Section four presents the results that relate to the questions and the initial purpose of the evaluation. This section most likely will contain tables, graphs, scores from tests, anecdotal summaries, and direct quotations.

5. The fifth section discusses the results presented in section four. Did the identification procedure identify students who benefit from the program? Do all students have equal access to the gifted and talented program using the current identification procedure? Were resources adequate for identifying gifted and talented students?

6. The final section includes a list of recommendations for the school district. Since this section may be the only one that is read by some of the audience, it needs to be written very carefully. Recommendations might be prioritized and also include options.

Action

Obviously, the final step for the school district is action. Which of the recommendations will be implemented? When? How? The school district has spent money in staff time and, perhaps, in contracting with an outside evaluator. The evaluation now provides an opportunity and a challenge to improve and strengthen the identification procedure so that all gifted and talented students are served.

References

Alvino, J., McDonnel, R., & Richert, S. (1981). National survey of identification practices in gifted and talented education. *Exceptional Children, 48,* 124–132.

American Educational Research Association, American Psychological Association, & National Council on Measurement in Education. (1999). *Standards for educational and psychological testing.* Washington, DC: American Educational Research Association.

Anastasi, A., & Urbina, S. (1997). *Psychological testing* (7th ed.). Upper Saddle River, NJ: Prentice-Hall.

Anthony, T. S. (1989, November). *Desegregation and gifted programs: What G/T coordinators should know.* Paper presented at the annual meeting of the National Association for Gifted Children, Cincinnati, OH.

Arter, J. (1990). *Using portfolios in instruction and assessment: State of the art summary.* Portland, OR: Northwest Educational Research Laboratory.

Baldwin (1973, March). *Identifying the disadvantaged.* Paper presented at the First National Conference on the Disadvantaged, Ventura, CA.

Bernal, E. (1981, February). *Special problems and procedures for identifying minority gifted students.* Paper presented at the annual meeting of the Council for Exceptional Children, New Orleans, LA.

Borland, J. H. (1989). *Planning and implementing programs for the gifted.* New York: Teachers College Press.

Borland, J. H., & Wright, L. (1994). Identifying young, potentially gifted, economically disadvantaged students. *Gifted Child Quarterly, 38,* 164–171.

Bracken, B. A., & McCallum, S. R. (1997). *Universal nonverbal intelligence test.* Itasca, IL: Riverside.

Brown, V. L., Hammill, D. D., & Wiederholt, J. L. (1995). *Test of reading comprehension* (3rd ed.). Austin, TX: PRO-ED.

Brown, L., Sherbenou, R., & Johnsen, S. (1997). *Test of nonverbal intelligence* (3rd ed.). Austin, TX: PRO-ED.

Camilli, G. (1993). The case against item bias detection techniques based on internal criteria: Do item bias procedures obscure test fairness issues? In P. W. Holland & H. Wainer (Eds.), *Differential item functioning* (pp. 397–413). Hillsdale, NJ: Erlbaum.

Carrow-Woolfolk, E. (1996). *Oral and written language skills.* Circle Pines, MN: American Guidance Services.

Cattell, R. B. (1963). Theory of fluid and crystallized intelligence: A critical experiment. *Journal of Educational Psychology, 54,* 1–22.

Clark, B. (1997). *Growing up gifted* (5th ed.). Upper Saddle River, NJ: Merrill.

Clark, G. A., & Zimmerman, E. (1984). *Educating artistically talented students.* Syracuse, NY: Syracuse University Press.

Colangelo, N., & Davis, G. A. (1991). *Handbook of gifted education.* Boston: Allyn and Bacon.

Coleman, L. J., & Cross, T. L. (2001). *Being gifted in school: An introduction to development, guidance, and teaching. Waco,* TX: Prufrock Press.

Coleman, M. R., Gallagher, J. J., & Foster, A. (1994). *Updated report on state policies related to the identification of gifted students.* Chapel Hill: University of North Carolina.

Connolly, A. J. (1998). *KeyMath revised.* Circle Pines, MN: American Guidance Services.

Cornish, R. L. (1968). Parents', pupils', and teachers' perceptions of a gifted child's ability. *Gifted Child Quarterly, 12,* 14–17.

CTB-Macmillan-McGraw-Hill. (1992). *California achievement test* (5th ed.). Monterey, CA: Author.

Csikszentmihalyi, M., Rathunde, K., & Whalen, S. (1993). *Talented teenagers: The roots of success and failure.* New York: Cambridge University Press.

Davis, G. A., & Rimm, S. B. (1994). *Education of the gifted and talented* (3rd ed.). Needham Heights, MA: Allyn and Bacon.

Denzin, N. K., & Lincoln, Y. S. (1994). *Handbook of qualitative research.* Thousand Oaks, CA: Sage.

Dunn, L. M., Dunn, L, M., Williams, K. T., & Wang, J. J. (1997). *Peabody picture vocabulary.* Circle Pines, MN: American Guidance Services.

Educational Testing Service. (1989). *Scholastic assessment test.* Princeton, NJ: Author.

Evans, C. S. (1993). When teachers look at student work. *Educational Leadership, 50*(5), 71–72.

Feldhusen, J. F., Asher, J. W., & Hoover, S. M. (1984). Problems in the identification of giftedness, talent, or ability. *Gifted Child Quarterly, 28,* 149–151.

Feldhusen, J. F., & Baska, L. K. (1985). Identification and assessment of the gifted and talented. In J. F. Feldhusen (Ed.), *Excellence in educating the gifted* (pp. 87–88). Denver: Love.

Feldhusen, J. F., Baska, L. K., & Womble, S. R. (1981). Using standard scores to synthesize data in identifying the gifted. *Journal for the Education of the Gifted, 4,* 177–185.

Feldhusen, J. F., Hoover, S. M., & Sayler, M. (1990). *Identifying and educating gifted students at the secondary level.* Monroe, NY: Trillium Press.

Feldt, L., Forsyth, R., Ansley, T., & Alnot, S. (1996). *Iowa tests of educational development: Forms K, L, and M.* Chicago: Riverside.

Ford, D. Y. (1996). *Reversing underachievement among gifted Black students: Promising practices and programs.* New York: Teachers College Press.

Frasier, M. (1987). Eliminating the four persisting barriers to identifying gifted students. *Gifted Students Institute Quarterly, 12*(3), 5–8.

Frasier, M. M. (1994). *A manual for implementing the Frasier Talent Assessment Profile (F-TAP): A multiple criteria model for the identification and education of gifted students.* Athens: Georgia Southern Press.

Frasier, M. M. (1997). Multiple criteria: The mandate and the challenge. *Roeper Review, 20*(2), 2–4.

143

Frasier, M., & Passow, A. H. (1994). *Toward a new paradigm for identifying talent potential* (Research Monograph 94112). Storrs: The National Research Center on the Gifted and Talented, University of Connecticut.

Gagné, F. (1995). From giftedness to talent: A developmental model and its impact on the language of the field. *Roeper Review, 18,* 103–111.

Gagné, F. (1999). Is there any light at the end of the tunnel? *Journal for the Education of the Gifted, 22,* 191–234.

Gagné, F., Bégin, J., & Talbot, L. (1993). How well do peers agree among themselves when nominating the gifted and talented? *Gifted Child Quarterly, 37,* 39–45.

Gardner, H. (1993). *Creating minds: An anatomy of creativity seen through the lives of Freud, Einstein, Picasso, Stravinsky, Eliot, Graham, and Gandhi.* New York: BasicBooks.

Geary, D. C., & Brown, S. C. (1991). Cognitive addition: Strategy choice and speed-of-processing differences in gifted, normal, and mathematically disabled children. *Developmental Psychology, 27,* 398–406.

Gear, G. (1978). Effects of training on teachers' accuracy in identifying gifted children. *Gifted Child Quarterly, 22,* 90–97.

Getzels, J. W., & Jackson, F. (1962). *Creativity and intelligence.* New York: Wiley.

Gilliam, J. E., Carpenter, B. O., & Christensen, J. R. (1996). *Gifted and talented evaluation scales.* Austin, TX: PRO-ED.

Ginsburg, H. P., & Baroody, A. J. (2003). *Test of early mathematics ability* (3rd ed.). Austin, TX: PRO-ED.

Goertzel, V., & Goertzel, M. G. (1962). *Cradles of eminence.* Boston: Little, Brown.

Gollnick, D. M., & Chinn, P. C. (1990). *Multicultural education in a pluralistic society* (3rd ed.). Upper Saddle River, NJ: Merrill/Prentice-Hall.

Grantham, T. C. (2003). Increasing Black student enrollment in gifted programs: An exploration of the Pulaski County Special School District's advocacy efforts. *Gifted Child Quarterly, 47,* 46–65.

Gregory, R. J. (2000). *Psychological testing: History, principles, and applications* (3rd ed.). Boston: Allyn and Bacon.

Gronlund, N. E. (1998). *Assessment of student achievement* (6th ed.). Needham Heights, MA: Allyn and Bacon.

Gruber, H. E. (1982). *Darwin on man: A psychological study of scientific creativity* (2nd ed.). Chicago: University of Chicago Press.

Guilford, J. P. (1950). Creativity. *American Psychologist, 5,* 444–454.

Hammill, D. D., & Larsen, S. C. (1996). *Test of written language* (3rd ed.). Austin, TX: PRO-ED.

Hammill, D. D., & Newcomer, P. L. (1997). *Test of language development: Intermediate* (3rd ed.). Austin, TX: PRO-ED.

Hammill, D. D., & Newcomer, P. L. (1997). *Test of language development: Primary* (3rd ed.). Austin, TX: PRO-ED.

Hammill, D. D., Pearson, N. A., & Wiederholdt, J. L. (1997). *Comprehensive test of nonverbal intelligence.* Austin, TX: PRO-ED.

Harcourt-Brace Educational Measurement. (1998). *Aprenda la prueba de logros en español* (2nd ed.). San Antonio, TX: Author.

Harcourt-Brace Educational Measurement. (1997). *Stanford achievement test* (9th ed.). San Antonio, TX: Author.

Hoover, H., Hieronymous, A., Frisbie, D., & Dunbar, S. (1993). *Iowa tests of basic skills: Forms K and L.* Chicago, IL: Riverside.

Hoover, H., Hieronymous, A., Frisbie, D., & Dunbar, S. (1996). *Iowa tests of basic skills: Form M.* Chicago: Riverside.

Houghton Mifflin Company. (1986). *Webster's II new college dictionary.* Boston: Author.

Hresko, W. P., Herron, S. R., & Peak, P. K. (1996). *Test of early written language* (2nd ed.). Austin, TX: PRO-ED.

Hresko, W. P., Reid, D. K., & Hammill, D. D. (1999). *Test of early language development* (3rd ed.). Austin, TX: PRO-ED.

Jacobs, J. (1971). Effectiveness of teacher and parent identification as a function of school level. *Psychology in the Schools, 8,* 140–142.

Jensen, A. (1969). How much can we boost IQ and scholastic achievement? *Harvard Educational Review, 39*(1), 1–24.

Johnsen, S. K. (1997). Assessment beyond definitions. *Peabody Journal of Education, 72,* 136–142.

Johnsen, S. K., & Corn, A. L. (2001). *Screening assessment for gifted elementary students* (2nd ed.). Austin, TX: PRO-ED.

Johnsen, S., & Ryser, G. (1994). Identification of young gifted children from lower income families. *Gifted and Talented International, 9*(2), 62–68.

145

Johnsen, S. K., & Ryser, G. R. (1997). The validity of portfolios in predicting performance in a gifted program. *Journal for the Education of the Gifted, 20,* 253–267.

Karnes, F. A. (1991). Leadership and gifted adolescents. In M. Bireley & J. Genshaft (Eds.), *Understanding the gifted adolescent* (pp. 122–138). New York: Teachers College Press.

Karnes, F. A., & Chauvin, J. C. (2000). *Leadership skills inventory.* Scottsdale, AZ: Gifted Psychology Press.

Karnes, F. A., & Marquardt, R. G. (1991). *Gifted children and the law.* Dayton: Ohio Psychology Press.

Kaufman, A. S., & Kaufman, N. L. (1993). *Kaufman adolescent and adult intelligence.* Circle Pines, MN: American Guidance Services.

Kaufman, A. S., & Kaufman, N. L. (1994). *Kaufman functional academic skills.* Circle Pines, MN: American Guidance Services.

Kaufman, A. S., & Kaufman, N. L. (1998). *Kaufman test of educational achievement: Normative update.* Circle Pines, MN: American Guidance Services.

Kerr, B. (1991). Educating gifted girls. In N. Colangelo & G. A. Davis (Eds.), *Handbook of gifted education* (pp. 402–415). Boston: Allyn and Bacon.

Kerr, B. (1994). *Smart girls two: A new psychology of girls, women, and giftedness.* Dayton: Ohio Psychology Press.

Khatena, J. (1988). *Multitalent assessment records.* Starkville: Mississippi State University.

Khatena, J. (1992). *Gifted: Challenge and response for education.* Itasca, IL: Peacock.

Khatena, J., & Morse, D. T. (1994). *Khatena-Morse multitalent perceptual inventory.* Bensenville, IL: Scholastic Testing Service.

Kitano, M. K. (1994/1995). Lessons from gifted women of color. *Journal of Secondary Gifted Education, 6,* 176–187.

Kubiszyn, T. W., & Borich, G. D. (2000). *Educational testing and measurement: Classroom applications and practice* (6th ed.). New York: Wiley.

Kurtz, B. E., & Weinert, F. E. (1989). Metacognition, memory performance, and causal attributions in gifted and average children. *Journal of Experimental Child Psychology, 48,* 45–61.

Laffoon, K. S., Jenkins-Friedman, R., & Tollefson, N. (1989). Causal attributions of underachieving gifted, achieving gifted, and nongifted students. *Journal for the Education of the Gifted, 13,* 4–21.

Linn, M., & Hyde, J. (1989). Gender, mathematics, and science. *Educational Researcher, 18*(8), 17–27.

Maccoby, E. E., & Jacklin, C. N. (1974). *The psychology of sex differences.* Stanford, CA: Stanford University Press.

Markwardt, F. C., Jr. (1997). *Peabody individual achievement test–Revised.* Circle Pines, MN: American Guidance Services.

McCarney, S. B., & Anderson, P. D. (1998). *Gifted evaluation scale* (2nd ed.). Columbia, OH: Hawthorne Educational Services.

McLouglin, J. A., & Lewis, R. B. (2001). *Assessing students with special needs* (5th ed.). Upper Saddle River, NJ: Merrill/Prentice-Hall.

Mills, C., Ablard, K. E., & Brody, L. E. (1993). The Raven's Progressive Matrices: Its usefulness for identifying gifted/talented students. *Roeper Review, 15,* 185–186.

Naglieri, J. A. (2003). *Naglieri nonverbal ability test.* San Antonio, TX: The Psychological Corporation.

Naglieri, J. A., & Ford, D. Y. (2003). Addressing underrepresentation of gifted minority children using the Naglieri Nonverbal Ability Test (NNAT). *Gifted Child Quarterly, 47,* 155–160.

Otis, A., & Lennon, R. (1996). *Otis-Lennon school ability test* (7th ed.). San Antonio, TX: Harcourt Brace Educational Measurement.

Ortiz, V., & Volkoff, W. (1987). Identification of gifted and accelerated Hispanic students. *Journal for the Education of the Gifted, 11,* 45–55.

Pegnato, C., & Birch, J. (1959). Locating gifted children in junior high schools: A comparison of methods. *Exceptional Children, 25,* 300–304.

Perkins, D. N. (1981). *The mind's best work.* Cambridge, MA: Harvard University Press.

Peterson, J. S., & Margolin, R. (1997). Naming gifted children: An example of unintended "reproduction." *Journal for the Education of the Gifted, 21,* 82–101.

Piirto, J. (1999). *Talented children and adults: Their development and education* (2nd ed.). Upper Saddle River, NJ: Merrill.

The Psychological Corporation. (1993). *Metropolitan achievement test* (7th ed.). San Antonio, TX: Author.

The Psychological Corporation. (2001). *Wechsler individual achievement test* (2nd ed.). San Antonio, TX: Author.

REFERENCES

Ramsey, P. A. (1993) Sensitivity review: The ETS experience as a case study. In P. W. Holland, & H. Wainer (Eds.), *Differential item functioning* (pp 367–388). Mahwah, NJ: Erlbaum.

Reid, D. K., Hresko, W. P., & Hammill, D. D. (2001). *Test of early reading ability* (3rd ed.). Austin, TX: PRO-ED.

Renzulli, J. S., Smith, L. H., White, A. J., Callahan, C. M., Hartman, R. K., & Westberg, K. L. (2002). *Scales for rating the behavioral characteristics of superior students.* Mansfield Center, CT: Creative Learning Press.

Richert, S. (1985). Identification of gifted children in the United States: The need for pluralistic assessment. *Roeper Review, 8,* 68–72.

Richert, S. (1991). Rampant problems and promising practices in identification. In N. Colangelo & G. A. Davis (Eds.), *Handbook of gifted education* (pp. 81–96). Needham Heights, MA: Allyn and Bacon.

Robinson, A., & Moon, S. M. (2003). A national study of local and state advocacy in gifted education. *Gifted Child Quarterly, 47,* 8–25.

Rogers, K. B. (2001). *Re-forming gifted education: Matching the program to the child.* Scottsdale, AZ: Great Potential Press.

Roid, G. H., & Miller, L. J. (1998). *Leiter international performance scale–Revised.* Wood Dale, IL: Stoetling.

Ryser, G. R., & Johnsen, S. K. (1998). *Test of mathematical abilities for gifted students.* Austin, TX: PRO-ED.

Ryser, G. R., & McConnell, K. (2004). *Scales for identifying gifted students.* Waco, TX: Prufrock Press.

Salvia, J., & Ysseldyke, J. E. (2001). *Assessment* (8th ed.). Boston: Houghton-Mifflin.

Sattler, J. M. (2001). *Assessment of children: Cognitive applications.* San Diego, CA: Sattler.

Scannell, D. P., Haugh, O. M., Lloyd, B. H., & Risinger, F. (1993). *Tests of achievement and proficiency: Forms K & L.* Chicago: Riverside.

Scannell, D. P., Haugh, O. M., Lloyd, B. H., & Risinger, F. (1996). *Tests of achievement and proficiency: Form M.* Chicago: Riverside.

Scruggs, T., & Mastropieri, M. (1985). Spontaneous verbal elaborations in gifted and nongifted youths. *Journal for the Education of the Gifted, 9,* 1–10.

Seashore, C. E., Leavis, D., & Saetveit, J. (1960). *Seashore measures of musical talents.* New York: Psychological Corporation.

Shaklee, B. D., Whitmore, J., Barton, L., Barbour, N., Ambrose, R., & Viechnicki, K. (1989). *Early assessment for exceptional potential for young and/or economically disadvantaged students.* Washington, DC: U.S. Department of Education , Office of Educational Research and Improvement.

Shambeck, V. R., Duncan, J., & Dougherty, E. (1988, September 23). *CIMA on wheels.* Lubbock, TX: Lubbock Independent School District.

Slosson, R. L., Nicholson, C. L., & Hibpshman, T. L. (1998). *Slosson intelligence test–Revised.* East Aurora, NY: Slosson Educational Publications.

Spearman, C. (1923). *The nature of "intelligence" and the principles of cognition.* London: Macmillan.

Stanley, J. (1976). The study of mathematically precocious youth. *Gifted Child Quarterly, 26,* 53–67.

Stanley, J. (1991). An academic model for educating the mathematically talented. *Gifted Child Quarterly, 35,* 36–41.

Sternberg, R. J. (Ed.). (1988). *The nature of creativity: Contemporary psychological perspectives.* Cambridge: Cambridge University Press.

Sternberg, R. J., & Davidson, J. E. (Eds.). (1986). *Conceptions of giftedness.* Cambridge: Cambridge University Press.

Stogdill, R. M. (1974). *Handbook of leadership: A survey of theory and research.* New York: Free Press.

Swassing, R. H. (1985). *Teaching gifted children and adolescents.* Columbus, OH: Merrill.

Tannenbaum, A. J. (1983). *Gifted children: Psychological and educational perspectives.* New York: Macmillan.

Texas Education Agency. (n.d.). *Non-traditional assessment of gifted students.* Austin, TX: Advanced Academic Services (formerly Division of Gifted/Talented Education).

Texas Education Agency (n.d.). *Texas student portfolio.* Austin, TX: Advanced Academic Services (formerly Division of Gifted/Talented Education).

Texas Education Agency, Division of Advanced Academic Services (1996). *Texas state plan for the education of gifted/talented students.* Austin, TX: Author.

Thorndike, R. L., & Hagen, E. P. (1997). *Cognitive abilities test: Form 5.* Chicago: Riverside.

Tolan, S. S. (1992a). Special problems of highly gifted children. *Understanding Our Gifted, 4*(3), 3, 5.

Tolan, S. S. (1992b). Parents vs. theorists: Dealing with the exceptionally gifted. *Roeper Review, 15,* 14–18.

Torrance, E. P. (1969). Creative positives of disadvantaged children and youth. *Gifted Child Quarterly, 13,* 71–81.

Torrance, E. P. (1974). *Torrance tests of creative thinking.* Bensenville, IL: Scholastic Testing Service.

Trice, B., & Shannon, B. (2002, April). *Office for Civil Rights: Ensuring equal access to gifted education.* Paper presented at the annual meeting of the Council for Exceptional Children, New York.

Trochim, W. (2000). *The research methods knowledge base* (2nd ed.). Cincinnati, OH: Atomic Dog.

U.S. Bureau of the Census. (2001). *The statistical abstract of the United States.* Washington, DC: Author.

U.S. Department of Education, Office of Educational Research and Improvement. (1993). *National excellence: A case for developing America's talent.* Washington, DC: U.S. Government Printing Office.

Wechsler, D. (2003). *Wechsler intelligence scale for children* (4th ed.). San Antonio, TX: The Psychological Corporation.

Whitmore, J. (1980). *Giftedness, conflict, and underachievement.* Boston: Allyn and Bacon.

Whitmore, J. (1981). Gifted children with handicapping conditions: A new frontier. *Exceptional Children, 48,* 106–114.

Winner, E. (1996). *Gifted children: Myths and realities.* New York: BasicBooks.

Woodcock, R. W. (1997). *Woodcock diagnostic reading battery.* Itasca, IL: Riverside.

Woodcock, R. W. (1998). *Woodcock reading mastery tests–Revised.* Circle Pines, MN: American Guidance Services.

Woodcock, R. W., McGrew, K., Mather, N., & Schrank, F. A. (2001). *Woodcock-Johnson III.* Chicago: Riverside.

Woodcock, R. W., McGrew, K. S., & Werder, J. E. (1994). *Woodcock-McGrewWerder mini battery of achievement.* Chicago: Riverside.

Zurcher, R. (1998). Issues and trends in culture-fair assessment. *Intervention in School and Clinic, 34,* 103–106.

Office for Civil Rights Checklist for Assessment of Gifted Programs

This document is designed to provide an overview of access concerns related to school districts' gifted programs. It is not intended as a standard of compliance with Title VI of the Civil Rights Act of 1964.

Statistical Analysis

❑ Racial/ethnic composition of the district's student enrollment.
❑ Racial/ethnic composition of student population receiving gifted services.
❑ Determine if minority students are statistically underrepresented in gifted programs. A statistically significant underrepresentation of minority students warrants a further, school-by-school, inquiry including statistical data/analyses regarding:
  ❑ Number (%) of students by race/ethnicity referred for evaluation for gifted eligibility.
  ❑ Number (%) of students by race/ethnicity determined eligible for gifted services.
  ❑ Number (%) of students by race/ethnicity withdrawing from, or otherwise discontinuing participation in, gifted programs/services.

Notice

❑ Is the notice of the gifted program, with respect to both content and method of dissemination, effective?

❏ Notice simply and clearly explains the purpose of the program, referral/screening procedures, eligibility criteria, and identifies the district's contact person.

❏ Notice is provided annually to students, parents, and guardians, in a manner designed to reach all segments of the school community.

Referral/Screening

❏ If there is a disparity in referral rates of minority students, determine if referral/screening practices and procedures are applied in a nondiscriminatory manner and if the district's practices and procedures provide equal access for all qualified students.

❏ Multiple alternative referral sources, e.g., teachers, parents, etc., are, in practice, accessible to and utilized by, all segments of the school community.

❏ Teachers and other district staff involved in the referral process have been trained and/or provided guidance regarding the characteristics of giftedness in general and special populations.

❏ Referral/screening criteria are applied in a nondiscriminatory manner.

❏ All referral/screening criteria/guidelines are directly related to the purpose of the gifted program.

❏ Standardized tests *and* cut off scores are appropriate (valid and reliable) for the purpose of screening students for gifted services.

Evaluation/Placement

❏ Are eligibility criteria and procedures applied in a nondiscriminatory manner and do they ensure equal access for all qualified students?

❏ Eligibility criteria are applied in a nondiscriminatory manner.

❏ Eligibility criteria are consistent with the purpose and implementation of the gifted program:

- Eligibility is based on multiple criteria.
- Criteria include multiple assessment measures.
- As appropriate, eligibility incorporates component test scores.

❑ Assessment instruments/measures and cut off scores are appropriate (valid and reliable) for the purpose of identifying students for gifted services

❑ To the extent that subjective assessment criteria are utilized, those individuals conducting the assessments have been provided guidelines and training to ensure proper evaluations.

❑ Alternative assessment instruments are utilized in appropriate circumstances.

❑ If private testing is permitted as the basis for an eligibility determination, it does not have a disparate impact on minority students or, if it does, the use of such testing is legitimately related to the successful implementation of the program and no less discriminatory alternative exists which would achieve the same objective.

Program Participation

❑ Are continued eligibility standards/criteria and procedures applied in a nondiscriminatory manner and do they ensure equal access for all qualified students?

❑ Continued eligibility standards/criteria are applied in a nondiscriminatory manner.

❑ Continued eligibility standards/criteria are consistent with the purpose and implementation of the gifted program.

❑ Implementation procedures and practices facilitate equal access for all students.

Program Implementation

❑ Are qualified minority students receiving the same quality of gifted programs and services?

❑ Programs and services are provided in locations that are comparably accessible to qualified students in predominantly minority schools.

❏ Qualified students at all of the district's schools receive gifted services/programs that are comparable with respect to quality *and* duration.

APPENDIX B

Statistical Tools: Converting Raw Scores to Standard Scores

Adapted from Issac, M., & Michael, W. (1971). *Handbook in research and evaluation*. San Diego, CA: EdITS.

Step 1. Begin with the raw scores. These are scores of 75 nominated students.

37	43	27	44	27	27	6	31	35	42	50
35	43	36	26	50	47	36	26	32	32	38
36	21	24	40	39	35	38	36	38	21	17
26	35	22	16	50	30	38	50	16	45	8
34	26	3	28	41	27	39	41	30	23	33
22	31	36	40	54	24	22	8	33	42	41
41	31	34	36	32	20	22	34	41		

Step 2. Identify the highest score and the lowest score. If there is a wide range, choose a class interval of 1, 2, 3, 10, 20, etc., and divide the range into classes of equal width. Seven to fifteen classes are desirable.

Highest score = 54; lowest score = 8; range = 47. Class interval of 5 will be used. (Note: the interval 50–54 is, in fact, 5 units wide: 50, 51, 52, 53, 54.

Step 3. Tally the number of cases with each score.

Step 4. Write the number of tallies in the Frequency (f) column. Add this column to get N, the number of cases.

Step 5. Select any interval, usually near the middle of the distribution. Call this the arbitrary origin. (Here, the 30–34 interval is used.) Determine the deviation (d) of each interval from the arbitrary origin.

Step 6. Multiply in each row the entries in the f and d columns, and enter in the fd column.

Step 7. Multiply the entries in the d and fd columns and enter in the fd2 columns. Add the fd and the fd2 columns. (Σ is a symbol meaning "sum of.")

Scores		(f)	d	fd	fd2
50–54	‖‖	5	4	20	80
45–49	‖	2	3	6	18
40–44	‖‖ ‖‖ ‖	12	2	24	48
35–39	‖‖ ‖‖ ‖‖ ‖	17	1	17	17
30–34	‖‖ ‖‖ ‖‖	14	0	0	0
25–29	‖‖ ‖‖	10	-1	-10	10
20–24	‖‖ ‖‖	10	-2	-30	40
15–19	‖	3	-3	-9	27
10–14		0	-4	-0	0
5–9	‖	2	-5	-10	50
		75		+18	290
		N		Σfd	Σfd2

Step 8. Substitute in the following formulas:

c (correction) = $\dfrac{\Sigma fd}{N}$ $c = \dfrac{18}{75} = .24$

M (mean) = A.O. $+ic^*$ M = 32.0 + 5(0.24) = 32.0 + 1.20 = 33.20

$$SD = i\sqrt{\dfrac{\Sigma fd2 - Nc^2}{N-1}} \quad SD = 5\sqrt{\dfrac{290 - 74(0.24)^2}{74}} = 5\sqrt{\dfrac{285.7}{74}}$$

$= 5\sqrt{3.86} = 5(1.96) = 9.80$

Step 9. To attain a z score for each raw score, use the following formula:

$$Z = \dfrac{X - M}{SD} = \dfrac{50 - 33.2}{9.8} = \dfrac{16.8}{9.8} = 1.71$$

In this example, a raw score of 50 is equal to 1.71. Looking at Table 5.4, 1.71 is approximately 125.5 (deviation IQ score), 96th percentile, 8th stanine, and in the superior range.

---

*A.O. is the midpoint of the score interval selected as arbitrary origin, and i is the width of the interval. SD is the standard deviation.

APPENDIX C

Statistical Tools: Calculating the Standard Error of Measurement

Adapted from Bruning, J., & Kintz, B. L. (1968). *Computational handbook of statistics.* Glenview, IL: Scott, Foresman.

To calculate the standard error of measurement, you will need to know the standard deviation (SD) and the reliability of the measure. After you have converted the raw scores to standard scores, you will have the standard deviation. The following list of steps will give you the reliability. You will then place the SD (standard deviation) and the r (reliability) into a formula to obtain the SEM (standard error of measurement.

Step 1. Calculating the reliability (Kuder-Richardson & Hoyt). Suppose that you wish to test the reliability of a certain test-item measure. For the purposes of determining reliability, record for each student on each test item whether the question was answered correctly (indicated by the number 1) or incorrectly (indicated by 0).

159

Sub.					Test Items					
	1	2	3	4	5	6	7	8	9	10
s1	1	1	1	1	1	1	1	1	1	1
s2	0	0	0	1	1	0	1	1	1	1
s3	0	0	1	1	1	0	0	0	0	0
s4	0	0	1	1	1	1	1	0	1	1
s5	0	1	1	1	1	0	1	0	1	1
s6	1	1	0	1	0	0	1	1	1	0
s7	0	0	1	1	0	0	1	0	0	1
s8	1	1	0	1	1	1	1	0	1	1

Step 2. Count the number of items that each student answered correctly. (In this example, 10 correct for the first student, 6, for the second student, etc.) List the total for each student.

Subject	No. of Correct Answers
s1	10
s2	6
s3	3
s4	7
s5	7
s6	6
s7	4
s8	8

Step 3. Add the number of correct answers (Step 2), and record the sum.

$$10 + 6 + 3 + 7 + 7 + 6 + 4 + 8 = 51$$

160

Step 4. Square each number of correct answers in Step 2; then add the squares and divide that sum by the number of items in the test (10 in this example).

$$\frac{10^2 + 6^2 + 3^2 + 7^2 + 7^2 + 6^2 + 4^2 + 8^2}{10} = \frac{359}{10} = 35.9$$

Step 5. Square the result of Step 3, and divide by the product of the number of people times the number of items (8 x 10 = 80 in this example).

$$\frac{51^2}{80} = \frac{2601}{80} = 32.512$$

Step 6. Subtract the result of Step 5 from the result of Step 3.

51 - 32.512 = 18.488

Step 7. Subtract the result of Step 5 from the result of Step 4.

35.9 - 32.512 = 3.388

Step 8. Count the number of subjects who correctly answered each item. List the totals for each item.

Item	No. of Persons Correct
1	3
2	4
3	5
4	8
5	6
6	3
7	7
8	3
9	6
10	6

Step 9. Square each number of persons correct in Step 8; then add the squares and divide that sum by the number of people who took the test (8 in this example).

$$\frac{3^2 + 4^2 + 5^2 + 8^2 + 6^2 + 3^2 + 7^2 + 3^2 + 6^2 + 6^2}{8} = \frac{289}{8} = 36.125$$

Step 10. Subtract the result of Step 5 from the result of Step 9.

36.125 - 32.512 = 3.613

Step 11. Subtract the result from Step 7 and the result from Step 10 from the result of Step 6.

18.488 - 3.388 - 3.613 = 11.487

Step 12. Divide the result of Step 7 by N - 1, where N is the number of subjects who took the test (8 in this example).

$$\frac{3.388}{N-1} = \frac{3.388}{8-1} = \frac{3.388}{7} = .484$$

Step 13. Divide the result of Step 11 by (N - 1)(I - 1), where N is the number of subjects who took the test (8 in our example) and I is the number of items in the test (10 in our example).

$$\frac{11.487}{(N-1)(I-1)} = \frac{11.487}{7 \times 9} = \frac{11.487}{63} = .182$$

Step 14. Subtract the result of Step 13 from the result of Step 12.

.484 - .182 = .302

Step 15. Divide the result of Step 14 by the result of Step 12. This yields the value of the Kuder-Richardson (or Hoyt) reliability coefficient.

$$\frac{.302}{.484} = .62$$

A reliability coefficient of .80 or higher would mean that the test was consistently measuring the same characteristic or trait (e.g., intelligence, creativity, mathematics, etc.). Substitute the Standard Deviation (SD) and the reliability (r) in the following formula to discover the standard error of measurement.

$$\text{SEM} = \text{SD} \sqrt{1-r} = 8 \sqrt{1-.62} = 8 \sqrt{.38} = 8 \times .62 = 4.96$$